GRA
ROOT OF DIVINE POWER

GRASPING THE ROOT OF DIVINE POWER

HRU YUYA.T. ASSAAN-ANU

ANU NATION

BEHIND ENEMY LINES

Grasping the Root of Divine Power
HRU Yuya T. Assaan-Anu
Anu Nation
www.AnuNation.org

HRU Yuya T. Assaan-ANU
"Grasping the Root of Divine Power"

© 2010, HRU Yuya T. Assaan-ANU
Anu Nation
www.AnuNation.org

ALL RIGHTS RESERVED. This book contains material protected under International and Federal Copyright Laws and Treaties. Any unauthorized reprint or use of this material is prohibited. No part of this book may be reproduced or transmitted in any form or by any means, electronic or mechanical, including photocopying, recording, or by any information storage and retrieval system without express written permission from the author / publisher.

Contents

Preface —• 7
Adimu —• 9
The One —• 11
Man and Wombmyn —• 17
Light and Lesser Light —• 21
Iwa Pele —• 29
Ase —• 33
What is Divination? —• 37
Who are we speaking to? —• 41
ORI —• 43
Egun/Lidlotis/Nananom Nsamanfo —• 46
Establishing your Gateway —• 53
Initiating the dialogue —• 65
OBI —• 77
Many faces of the OBI —• 81
Kola nut —• 85
Opening the world of the OBI Abata —• 86
"ANU OBI" —• 89
Medicinal uses for the OBI/Coconut: —• 90
5 the Hard Way —• 95
The Casting Surface —• 107
And the whole 9! —• 119
Orisa —• 135
The 7 Afrakan Powers —• 143
So Fresh and So Clean clean! —• 173
Conclusion —• 181
Glossary —• 185

Preface

Firstly, this work is written from a Pan-Afrakan perspective and makes no attempts to universalize the concepts being presented but, rather represents an effort to establish a sense of collectivism and Umoja amongst the dispersed Afrakans who desire to align themselves with the one culture and life calculation that resides in all people of Afrakan ascent. Afrakan culture is of one aim and purpose although expressed through a multitude of ethnicities.

Researching the methods described in this book are just a cog in the wheel that one must implement on the journey of discovering "**How to be an Afrakan**".

Equally, when I speak of being an Afrakan, I am referring to the blood lineage, spiritual inheritance, and concepts associated with the continent of Afrika/Akebulon.

Expectantly I can claim this as my blood and birthright because I am a spiritual, familial, biological, geographical, and cultural product of Afraka. I am also a melaninated individual with a natural Afrakan crown.

Manifesting the dynamic spirit of OUR combined desire to comprehend "us" is high aspiration. This work is the 1st in a series outlining the "Black-print" needed to follow in order to Re-Afrakanize and reclaim OUR stolen/forgotten legacy. I see it fit that the series commence with instruction on establishing a proper spiritual base; as all things initiate in the spirit realm and then manifest in the realm of condensed matter. We cannot heal as a people without our linkage to the *Great Spirit*.

In reading you'll find this work leans heavily on the Yoruba Ifa tradition in language and conceptual expression. This is not an assertion of one Afrakan system over another but, is a result of me being primarily a student of Ifa. I am a Pan-Afrakanist and I am in love with all Afrakan traditional spiritual systems. They are all equally ingrained in my consciousness.

Naturally, the ideas that I'm presenting, as with much of this work, are of my own cognition birthed from meditation, research, and divine communion. You will, no doubt, hear varied opinions and perspectives as it relates to Afrakan spirituality and the realization of the Sankofa charge. Your ORI will guide.

Delve into the concepts presented in this book and push them to your limits. Divine Power is an integral link in the chain of survival and cultural continuance for US as a people. Without an unyielding grasp on OUR own original spiritual laws, we are drifting further out - into a sea of cultural amnesia and demise. We must know our Ancestors and be them!

Adimu

First this is a word offering to my Egun and Lidlotis:
My Great Grandmamma Laura Nelms, Grand Baba Carrie Stinson, Grandmamma Gladys Stinson, Uncle Walter, and Grand Aunt Viola.
Every time this book is read may you be honored and elevated.

And then....
I give honor and Ra-spect to my Grand Baba Robert Lee, my Grand Mama Gertrude Lee-McBride, My Abu - Baba Jeremiah, My Mama Olumoola Adejola, Aunt Irene, Cousin Diane, Brother Omar, Brother Ali, Sis-Star Syediah, Uncle J.R., My instructor Baba Olaoluwa Fasade and his light bearer Mama Osunsina Fasade, Mwalimu K. Bomani Baruti and Akoben House for the love and insight and to all those whose work towards my transformation, healing, and ascension.

To my beautiful, spiritual, deep, and loving daughter... Asaata. Baba gives this book to you, "Baby Girl". You are my greatest work and through you the wombmyn of the world will witness the majesty of Afraka.

This is a work for all my children, biological and spiritual, born and unborn.
To the wombmyn who radiate and carry my light........
Nakapenda.

Ase Ase Ase O!!!

ADIMU

HRU Assaan-Anu

The One

Abode santann yi firi tete; obi nte ase a onim ne ahyease, na obi ntena ase nkosi neawie, GYE NYAME.

This great panorama of creation dates back to time immemorial; no one lives who saw its beginning and no one will live to see its end, EXCEPT Oboadee (Creator), Nyame (Supreme Intelligence), Odomankoma (Infinite, Inventor), Ananse Kokuroko(The Great Spider; The Great Designer)

"01"

The one-

Everything has its origin in "The one". There is none that can be conceived greater.

When working with Orisa and Protector spirits we are working to navigate our way through this world and better comprehend our place and role in it. We don't send request to "The One"… only worship. We strive to exemplify the enormity that "The One" has breathed into us by working with the Orisa divinities that have been provided to us as guides and assistants on this life journey.

I'll use the numerical expression of "01" to refer to this Supreme Being as within this number sequence we see a hidden science of creation. The "0" represents everything and nothing all at once. It is the all inclusive cipher; the womb of the Black Wombmyn. The "1" represents the driving intention that brings itself into being through its will to move forward. The "1" is the male phallus that brings inspired purpose to the "0". Man and Wombyn. So, when we think of "The One" or "The Supreme Being" we should always distinguish that there is no Mfalme (King) without a Malika (Queen), no Sango without Oya, no Tehuti without Ma'at.

We worship the supreme "01" and give the proper tribute through our Ofo Ase (word power) but, our Adimu (offerings) and Ebo go to the Orisa and Egun. The "01" does not deal with the fulfillment of our desires though the "01" oversees the entities that do.

I'm using this term "01" for more than a few reasons. I'm a pan-Afrakanist and I'm in love with the land mass that birthed the highest ideas of my cultural inheritance. For me the "One" is "Unkulunkulu" as noted in Zulu land, "Tummu" as noted by

Grasping the Root of Divine Power

my Ethiopian family, "Omakongo" and "Nzambi Mpungu" as noted by my family in the Kongo, "Ra" as noted by the family along the Nile River Valley or more properly named TA-Meri, or "Oludumare" from the family in Nigeria. For the purpose of wide-ranging Afrakan inclusiveness, I'll use "**01**".

As warrior scholars we strive towards cultural reclamation/purity despite knowing many of our traditional spiritual systems have been tainted by the reports and misinterpretations from early Christian missionary's and other equally wicked minded invaders obedient to their cultural imperative. Themes of the all male trinity, the devil, and even a blissful afterlife proceeding a lifetime of anticipated affliction have been superimposed over our original life calculations. Prior to the enslavement process waged by Asian, Arab, and European invaders there had been many years of cultural onslaught on our long-established systems; by these same groups. This should be noted when reconsidering the concept of a Supreme Being. The truth is, as an Afrakan, you are much closer to that Almighty entity than "His-Story" has ever informed you. The only way your mind could have ever conceptualized the idea of a "God" is for you to have already acknowledged , inwardly, that you *are* that "God".

We fight to reconcile our ways and actions with the original moral code that was imparted to us at our moment before launch into this world of touch, sense, beginnings and endings. Our source is that Supreme organism of abundance and immeasurable creative possibilities that we've tricked ourselves/been tricked into believing is "10 zillion light years away". As a result we suffer from feelings of lack, creative blockages, doubt, identity crisis, and a myriad of dis-eases related to spiritual dispossession.

"01"

In this life we're gifted an enormous amount of spiritual backing; all to strike a chord and remind us how to dance once again to the universal *downbeat*. To be in step with the cosmic rhythm is the aim of all spiritualist and those who work with the force of the Egun/Lidlotis/Nananom Nsamanfo.

I began playing instruments at the age of 7 and still am an active musician to this day. I conceptualize the majority of my world through my two primary arts; music and martial sciences.

Question:

Have you ever noticed how Afrakans (continental and diasporic) clap to music as opposed to non-Afrakans?

I've always noticed that Afrakans, when listening to music in 4/4 time signature, always clap on the "2 and 4"; whereas non-Afrakans clap on the "1 and 3". So, if the music has a "Boom-pap-Boom-Boom-pap" rhythm; The Afrakans will clap on the "pap"/"2 and 4" whereas the non-Afrakans clap on the "Boom"/"1 and 3". I deduce this is because Afrakan feel the "1" they don't have to interrupt it...they let it breathe and they respond to the one with a clap. Non-Afrakans, more often than not, have "God Complexes" and want to be the "01", so they clap (superimpose themselves) over the "01"/"Boom"/"Downbeat". This is one case in point out of many describing how OUR relationship to the "01" manifest itself.

Traveling the continent of Akebulon in concept and admiration we discover one cultural substructure that serves as pedestal for the multitudinous ethnic expressions. Akebulon host many different ethnic groups but, there is one Afrakan Culture. The same can be said for European culture; no matter if it expresses itself in French, Spanish, German, or Italian the objectives and actions seem to be the same throughout the planet. One need only look at the tracks left by this group culture to prove this assertion (colonialism, globalization, imperialism, capitalism, racial decimation, the institution of suicidal culture, ceaseless warring, enslavement of indigenous people, KWK...).

We must stand guard like tireless sentinels at the gateway of OUR own minds with a vigilant warrior's posture; scrutinizing and dissecting any external imposition of the concept of the "01". This life should be a return to your greatness. The "01" is the destination of that return and will not be found in any "New Age" or "New and Improved" neocolonial African philosophy. This awareness resides within you. If your method for spiritual adoration and devotion moves you away from the doctrine of your Ancestors, it is toxic and will only bring calamity, spiritual lunacy, and cultural desolation. Do not be fooled by a people who have nothing to give you but, regurgitated, misunderstood religion...that they don't even *believe* anymore. Do not dance to their stiff claps on the "1 and 3" but, feel the **Boom** of the universal downbeat as the "01" still calls you to it. Realize that your natural way of living is the basis for all world religions and truth seekers. Afrakan, YOU are the earthly reflection and reproduction/RAproduction of the "01". Your life is on display.

So if you don't know, now you know.

Man and Wombmyn

Adherence to the laws of male and female energy is vital to innerstanding the regenerative workings of this galaxy; as these are complementary energies that work to manifest all that we know, see, here, touch, and feel.

MAN AND WOMBMYN

It's a Man's world-

This is a statement not far from the truth told by the legendary Godfather of soul. The masculine energy is the mystical initial idea of a force. It is the innovative will of light that synthesizes with the undifferentiated matter of darkness in order to bring forth a corporeal reality. It is the thought behind the expression. The masculine force is the will and drive of spiritual energy. It is the rational logic and mental magic of thought. Masculine energy is the instigating force in all things.

During sexual intercourse the male holds seeds of light within him (sperm) that possess boundless potential (and yes, within sperm is actual light). This is liquid light.

Masculine energy is a fiery expansive provoking force that is most comfortable when allowed to expand itself in the outer-sphere. The light of the Sun/Son...photosynthesis distributes information. Information is knowledge, not wisdom. Knowledge is the fundamental building block of life and ALL transformation.

Knowledge is information or rather "Inform-Atum"...informing The "Creator". Kemetic account states Atum created Shu and Tefnut by having sexual intercourse with Iusaaset.

Atum in Kemetic tradition is recognized as the setting Sun. In physical vision what does the Sun set into? The dark abysmal waters are the receptor of the setting Sun. The waters are the feminine element expressed through nature.

"Atum" represents the 1st in creation. This is another concept borrowed/stolen by non-Afrakans as portrayed in the mythological Bible story of "Adam and Eve". It is also reflected in the term "Atom"; which refers to the smallest unit of measurement where measurement begins.

But, it wouldn't be nothing without a wombmyn!-
What good is a world with no soul?
What good is a seed with no soil to incubate it?
What good is light without a cradle of darkness to contain it?

Let's get into it.

Feminine energy is the matter of all creation. It is the water or darkness that receives fire and light and sculpts it into the form that the light initially wills.

As in the previous intercourse example, the darkness holds the boundless potential of what could be but, also serves as the holder of the mystery of what *will* be. In darkness lives all mystery but, in darkness all solutions are unearthed.

Communication between the soul and spirit is only possible through feelings. The wombmyn or feminine energy is the gateway to the spirit world. Therefore, when we refer to womanly influence we are speaking of psychic gateways; the power to motivate spirit to action through the use of feelings. The soul begins where the nervous system ends.

Feminine energy is represented as wisdom because the soul maintains the imprint of past experience. The work of the wombmyn is to clear past experience programming.

This female energy is also a contracting force that herds light. Feelings are gatherers of light. Wombmyn gathers the materials that are needed to form the new human inside of her.

Feminine energy is a cool, calming energy; at its zenith of potency when "at home". Receptivity is its gift.

MAN AND WOMBMYN

Light and Lesser Light
The science of Light and Dark

LIGHT AND LESSER LIGHT

Lights on....Lights Out!!
The science of Light and Dark

Comprehension of the concept of light and dark are imperative in order to truly grasp the manner in which the divination oracles communicate with us.

The concepts of light/dark bring with them their own "sub-concepts" that reveal the duality, or even multiplicity, that's expressed by these elements.

Light it up Ras!

Light: Male, Fire, Active Force, Active Will, Visible Manifestation, Forward Motion, Blinding

Light is a force that we derive from fire. Make no mistake, with no fire there is no light.

Light is synonymous with our active will to create.

To explain further:

Light is the stimulate that propels and regulates all life on earth. For example: Sunlight feeds and strengthens the First Eye; commonly referred to as the Third eye or pineal gland. The Pineal gland/First Eye regulates the rhythm of our bodily organs, the processing of vitamin D received from the sun, the maintenance of skin pigmentation as determined by our melanin content, and a host of other functions. Most significantly, through our First Eye vision we are able to see beyond the mundane and mentally create whatever we desire to materialize on the physical plain. This ability to truly "see" is strengthened through interaction with sunlight. This "seeing" drives our will to create.

Not only should you stop bringing forth Afrakan babies out of your Wombs in hospitals but, they should never come forth under fluorescent lighting as it confuses the First eye.

LIGHT AND LESSER LIGHT

With Light comes ire (blessings) but, gifts from the spirit world come in various forms. Light illuminates our surroundings and exposes hidden danger but, light also allows us to see the divine endowments that surround us.

Conversely, light can be blinding and a lack of RAspect for this strong element can cause one to become disoriented. Too much light can burn us to the root.

For example:

If you were to plant a flower and decided you'd like to place that flower on your fire escape for the entire neighborhood to see; and in effect expose it to the fullness of the sun; if that flower was not properly rooted in the soil (unseen), it would burn and wilt. It's the investment and nurturing in what is unseen that allows us to fully accept the blessing of the light. Remember, a tree has more roots than branches.

As we advance in our learning of the U-N-I-verse, often our zeal leads us to want to share all that we've discovered with those we feel might benefit from our new found information. Just like the sun, we have to calculate just how much light to give the recipients of that information, as that illumination could quickly turn from an energizing nutritious force into a scorch that could burn up those we'd like to receive our message. With great knowledge comes great responsibility (notice I didn't say wisdom).

Too Black, Too Strong:

AWO DUDU

Dark: Female, Water, Undifferentiated Matter, Limitless Potential, Unseen, Protection, Blockage, Blinding

Darkness can represent the dark behaviors and habits that we keep secret. Darkness also serves as a great protectorate.

The mysteries of existence reside in the dark but enlightenment is also born out of that same dark matter. When a wombmyn is carrying a child in her womb there is a wondering and mystery that exist surrounding the specifics of the child that she is expecting. In that dark womb the child is completely protected and provided for. Whatever that child needs it is able to convey on a bio-spiritual level to its host and the host provides it.

When the child emerges from its mother's womb the mystery that was held now is brought to light while that same darkness that once cradled the child returns to its original form. Darkness is undifferentiated matter.

Darkness is the latent potentiality of the expanding U-N-I-verse. As your knowledge expands so does the circumference of the U-N-I-verse in order to accommodate thought to material

LIGHT AND LESSER LIGHT

manifestation.

So in this example we see that the darkness provided a cradle for the light that it held within its protective walls.

Darkness in divination can also represent a blockage of some sort. It's important for us to note that a blockage is not always the work of some outside force but, more often than not a result of something we are consciously or super-consciously holding onto that has outgrown its purpose in our lives.

There are times when you'll interpret darkness as danger and you'll be absolutely correct in that calculation; as what we ***do not know*** can hurt us. Danger can loom in dark places and often energies that attempt to do us harm perform their best work in the places that we do not attempt to illuminate. This does not automatically imply that they have any power to actually affect our lives adversely beyond the degree that we ***allow***.

One could hide behind a tree, unbeknownst to a nearby crowd of people and throw a stone into the middle of that crowd of people and then retreat to a "safe" unseen place. This is the action of a coward and clearly not one who is manifesting an active formidable power.

Comparisons can be made between the warrior personality who boldly makes their approach and mixes no words; attacking head on or one who uses an indirect approach. Mike Tyson or Muhammed Ali......you pick. Head on or rope-a-dope you can still get banged up.

Ovastand the sleek beauty, gracefulness of all things dark and respect its ability to shift the balance of things without even a clue of its presence.

LIGHT AND LESSER LIGHT

Iwa Pele

Iwa Nikan L'osoro o
Iwa Nikan L'osoro
Ori kan ki buru lout ife
Iwa Nikan L'osoro O

Character is all that is requisite
Character is all that is requisite
There is no destiny to be called unhappy in Ife City
Character is all that is requisite

- Orunmila

IWA PELE

Iwa Pele is one of the most vital attributes you could strive for through this process of "living".

It's commonly stated that "Iwa Pele", translated into English would translate as "Good Character" or "Gentle Character".

In fact this phrase does not mean "good" character. Neither one of these words translate into "good". The Yoruba phrase for good character is "Iwa Rere".

Iwa Pele is an abbreviated version of the phrase "Iwa Ope ile" meaning "I come to greet the Earth". So, in essence to have Iwa Pele is to have reverence for the earth. What group in the Afrakan village is physically greeted and revered above all? OUR Elders! We are all children of the earth (the greatest material Elder).

Why is this notion so crucial? Facing nature is the act of living in harmony with it. Living outside of the laws and wishes of nature creates a wickedness that not only blocks the fortune of life but, hinders your ability to connect with the forces that provide guidance and who speak through whatever oracle it is that you're using. We could explore this concept in many volumes as to the methods and ancients norms that cultures have developed in order to live in harmony with their natural surroundings but, it would be a bit too exhaustive to delve further in this work.

RAspect Nature and live according to the natural laws of the U-N-I-verse.

Iwa Pele brings spiritual protection (even from "hexes and curses") and increased Ase. When you are in alignment with the natural forces of the earth you are then able to call upon and even ride the current of those forces.

So, you've wondered "how can I get Orisa to respond to my prayers"? Iwa Pele - proper reverence of their earthly manifestations as expressed in nature.

I'll give you an example.......

One day, I was instructed to give Adimu (offering) to Osun. At that time I had very little to give, in terms of material offering; so, I went to a stream not far from where I lived armed with a few plastic bags. There were all kinds of beer cans, paper, and rubbish in and around a particular stream. I cleaned the stream thoroughly for about 100 feet upstream and downstream. Afterwards I said my Oriki (invocation) Osun over the water and area that I had cleaned and thanked Mama Osun for presenting me with an opportunity to uncover her beauty. This served as my Osun offering and an exercise in Iwa Pele (reverencing nature).

This is, in my opinion, the single greatest aspiration one could have in their ambition to comprehend nature's language and commune with it for the purposes of divination.

If you're querying your Egun/Lidlotis/Nananom Nsamanfo remember the rocks, minerals, plant life, animal life, and earth elements are your Ancestors. So strive to be the highest ideas and aspirations of your Egun/Lidlotis/Nananom Nsamanfo and your spiritual work will reflect your commitment to this dear planet and the life that it sustains for us all.

Side note: This is a very important conceptual reference when you're trying to judge the effectiveness or integrity of a reading, someone you'd potentially have read you, judgments concerning "Houses" to join, and Elders who you may be considering to do "work" for you. You should ask yourself the question, "what am I picking up about the character of this person?". Bad character of a diviner taints the accuracy of their readings.

IWA PELE

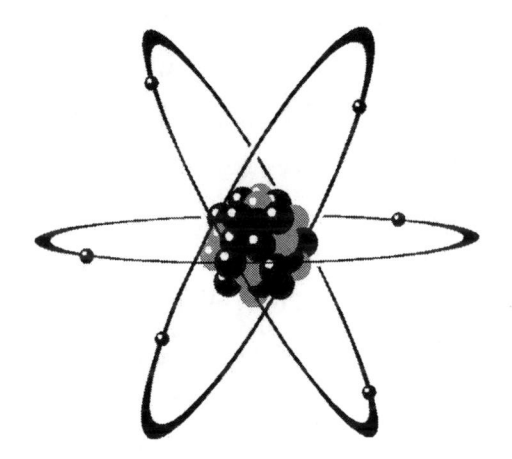

Ase

ASE

Ase-

We all have ASE...it is one's inborn power. Every element, mineral, plant, and living species has its own frequency of ASE.

Ase is the authority, strength, and vital nucleic power in all things. Ase is the energy of manifestation and procreation. It is the inner life force that also endorses the authority granted by how one lives or what they proclaim.

It is through our portion of Ase we manifest and coordinate the greater universal energies that are also manifestations of the same Ase that we are comprised of. Developing your personal Ase will grant you the power to truly construct/reconstruct reality. Ase has the privilege and ability to manifest itself through varied mediums and expressions. With Ase we transform word into physical materialization.

Electromagnetic energy (thought) becomes condensed matter through the focus of attention and word power. This is the solidification of Ase into the realm that we call reality.

Ase ,the power of manifestation, often is defined as "So it will be". Ase is the foundational power that all things in existence possess (rivers, mountains, streams, rocks, walking people, crawling people, swimming people, flying people, words, fire, wind, kwk...).

Ways you can develop your Ase are through good character, deep breathing, tantric activities, optimum health, eating a live food live-et, prayer, and ritual work.

When we call upon the Orisa to carry out a task we need Ase in order to invoke them and to give them the needed vehicle of travel from Orun to Aye; the invisible to the tangible. The Orisa, when properly utilized, are manufacturers of Ase. Many will employ the

Ase of Oriki's, Ofo Ase, blood, organic matter, water, kwk...

Ase is the active force of the universe that permeates every cell of everything...even the book you are currently holding has its own Ase. All things have an innate power that can even be borrowed from for the purpose of conducting the unseen forces to manifest a preferred reality.

When we look at the process of "Animal Sacrifice"; we need to look at it from the Afrakan perspective. Ebo's (a more complete word describing what is mistakenly referred to as "sacrifice") involving animals that belong to certain Orisa are designed to utilize the blood of that being in order to transform energy. The meat of the animal is customarily used to feed the greater KEM-unity. Blood is the river of light and life. Blood facilitates transmission of bio-spiritual awareness (This is Osun's realm).

Blood is liquid Ase.

*Ase is not equivalent to the word "Amen". If we were to correlate "Amen" to our own origins we'd have to see it as a manifestation of the word "Amon"; our reference to the unseen aspects of the supreme creator "Ra" (Amon-Ra). "Amon-Ra" governs the 97% percent of creation that remains unseen to the physical eye but is evidently present. So, after a prayer asking for assistance or protection from an unseen but, known place it would be logical to end it with the acknowledgement of the unseen power of the universe "Amon". It is not identical to "Amen" but, sheds light as to the true origins of the word "Amen".

ASE

What is Divination?

DIVINATION

What is Divination?

Divination is the act of connecting with Nature or that which is considered sacred.

Through the process you are connecting with the elements that are considered to be "divine". Divine elements are those that are thought of to be natural or in simpler terms, pertaining to *"God". I consider that a simplified definition as there is much on this planet that pertains to "God" but, sadly much of it goes amiss by many of its inhabitants.

Through the process of divination we are tuning into different frequency's that exist around us in order to commune with them. Through this communion we are granted access to a knowing that would otherwise not be accessible to our corporeal facilities.

The more we engage in the process, the more we become like the very energy's or entities that we are seeking guidance from. Their mind becomes our mind and we find our place on life's stage discovering our sonic contribution to the universal orchestral harmony.

Communing with nature (hiking, swimming, observing wildlife) allots us opportunities to sharpen the ability to see the divine message that's conveyed through all objects. I've learned my greatest lessons from trees, small crawling people, flowing water, and nature sounds.

You can peer out your window now and observe the humility of the trees. You'll see that some of the smaller branches of the trees aim straight up and reach for the sun while the larger ones take a more lateral or horizontal growth path.

We can deduce that there are times when you'll have to stoop or humble yourself in order to continue to grow or RAspect the weight of your wisdom because improperly measured, it can cause you to break from your root and fall to the ground to wither. By making a lateral movement you also give the younger ones behind you an opportunity to stand on your shoulders and push the collective mission, as programmed through your root DNA, to advance.

So, as I see it, divination is the process of seeing the message and unseen foundational intention in all of nature.

Though this work gives instructional for OBI divination, you'll see that the focus is on the process of cultivating ones intuition and recognizing the, sometimes subtle, clues that are to be found in interacting with any natural divine element. Once there is an ovastanding of how these elements inter-operate with one another and one's own nature, the reader will be able to draw up a more personal and functional OBI interpretation for themselves.

Through divination we'll see how the manifestation of thoughts, ideas, and willpower leaves the eternal realm (Orun) and enters the temporal realm (Aye) and the different ways they are expressed.

*I use the term here God for parenthetical reference but, it is not a term that I consider to be in proper place when one is looking to truly grasp traditional Afrakan nature systems as "God" is a Greek word and holds a connotation that doesn't encapsulate the idea of a Supreme Afrakan intelligence or deity in Afrakan terms. For example: The terms "God" and Olodumare are not interchangeable.

DIVINATION

Who are we speaking to?

THE SAGES

So who's providing the answers?

When divining there are many different sources that one could tap into in order to receive the answers that are needed but, in this work we'll focus on two; the ORI and the EGUN.

I do not recommend casting to the Orisa unless you are properly instructed on how to do so and can interpret the messages relayed by those energies.

Also, there is often way too much focus on connecting with energies that are perceived to be external to one's own self (though the Orisa live within and without). This has been a detrimental diversion from the original tenants of Afrakan spirituality wherein it was known that all things exist internally and externally. Revered was the high the discipline of "knowledge of self".

So, let us begin with the ORI.

ORI

Your own personal Superhru...I mean "Super-Hero"....

Here is where we find one of the greatest distinguishing aspects between Afrakan spirituality and western religion. With the Yoruba aspect of the Ori, it is noted that we are all birthed into this world accompanied by a personal guardian Orisa who, in fact, is our truest self; the source of our energy. Your ORI is YOU and YOU are your ORI.

This is ours to have and takes no acceptance of its presence or ritual that cleanses us from the "impurity" of our conception as a result of the sin of Man entering the course of Wombmyn.

Your ORI holds the portion of divinity and destiny that you were appropriated in Orun (Heaven) prior to your arrival here in Aye (Earth). It is your individualized ration of the supreme consciousness that maintains the motion of the universe. It is commonly stated, in regards to ORI, that it is the container for a person's destiny and that destiny is predetermined in Orun.

It is the author's deduction that a person's ORI represents more of a preordained path rather than a predestined path. A predestined path would be one that would not require effort on the part of the owner of that Ori (head).

For example:

If one is predestined to be a person of great notoriety and success and live a life of opulence and comfort. Then it would be logical to presuppose that individual would not have to do anything to support or motivate the materialization of that type of existence.

Your Ori is positioned at your crown, brow, and navel chakra points, to name a few.

Your Ori is will/drive but, has not character. Your Ori defers to the various Orisa consciousness in order to express itself with the most appropriate character in a given situation. For instance, if your Ori deems it necessary for you to face a situation in order to move from fear to fearlessness it may utilize the Sango consciousness in order for it to accomplish what is desired. The Sango consciousness will serve as the vehicle for character while the Ori is the propulsion of manifestation for that Sango force.

Your Ori has multiple aspects that all function in coalition with one another:

Ori - Your conscious mind
Ara- Your physical body temple
Ori Inu- This is your inner-self; your super conscious mind
Ipako - This is your connection to your extended family
Iponri- This is your true spirit body that resides in Orun
Iwaju- This is your 1st eye; Your clairvoyant portal
Atari- Transcendent cognition that connects you to your spirit self in Orun

Our ORI assist us in achieving oneness with all of creation while maintaining and strengthening our relationship with our highest order thinking and functioning.

Our ORI is our chain link to the supreme intelligence. It is our individualized portion of Oludumare's divine spark which allows us to fully realize ourselves as deities.

It is the paramount self and the superconscious. One can connect to the Ori through meditation and rituals similar to connecting with the ORI-sa.

Interestingly in the TV series "Stargate" there's a group of "god-like" alien antagonist called the "Ori". They have paranormal abilities and powers that allow them to represent themselves as "Gods". They live on another plain of existence and profess to have a direct connection to the supreme power of the universe.

These individuals originally came with a doctrine of peace from their sacred scriptures "The Book of *Origin*" but, later were exposed to have a more sinister destructive agenda. The Ori have ambassadors called "prios" who serve as their religious evangelist; traveling across the galaxy spreading their doctrine. This is needed because the Ori are incapable of directly affecting the material universe. Sound familiar? Can you say *Manifest Destiny*?

*This series has many themes that are meant to distort the Afrakan legacy and culture. I would strongly advise against using it as an OURstorical Afrakan reference but, it is interesting to note how OUR original concepts are utilized to mix much deception in with a base truth. This leads to cultural misorientation.

THE SAGES

Egun/Lidlotis/Nananom Nsamanfo

"Atunwa" - *The Yoruba concept of reincarnation. We are perpetually returning to a reality on earth that we previously helped to create.*

Who do you think led you to reading this work?
What led you to explore the deeper aspects of your own spirit and body?

Our Ancestors...the shoulders on which we stand.

Your Ancestors are always whispering wisdom in your ear; always calling you to advance the objectives of your bloodline.

It should be noted that regardless of what tradition you observe or have an affinity for; as an Afrakan there are certain fundamental concepts you must know when honoring those that have transcended to the next stage.

Your Ancestors are the empathic link between the corporeal realm and the spirit world as they have the compassion to have full innerstanding of what it is you are feeling and the emotions you are conveying when you commune with spirit for they have felt it and lived it themselves. Eternal spirit deities do not possess the same level of sensory access as those living in the physical realm or who *have* lived in the physical realm.

Being "dead" is not sufficient requisite for being a revered Egun/Lidlotis/Nananom Nsamanfo. The things you do during your physical existence will affect your standing once you transition. I do not subscribe to the notion that all beings who have transcended this life are worthy of honor or can serve as appropriate consulting sources for the purposes of divination.

Life is an upwards spiral....not a circle of redundancy. What this means is there's always opportunity for ascension, development, and growth; regardless of the plain of existence one resides.

For example, it would be foolish to imagine that one who lived a durational, unenlightened, anti-Afrakan existence while here in Aye (earth) would immediately be completely aware of the mysteries of existence because they experience the transformation of physical death. In kind, it would be equally foolish to imagine that someone of this sort would have the same wisdom to impart from the Ancestral realm as someone who manifested a life of enlightenment, knowledge, wisdom, and innerstanding and served as Jegna to their respective come-unity while on Aye.

When time comes to divine who would you rather dialog with?

The difference between an Egun/Lidlotis/Nananom Nsamanfo and dead people can be likened to the difference between an Elder and an "Old Person". Character is the key word of the day..... every day.

Every old person is not an Elder or even mature. Anyone who is not supporting your Re-Afrakanization process, and the reclaiming of your right mind, is your enemy and should be handled as such.

The Ancestors that we should strive to embody and connect with should be recognized as the following:
- Those that were KEM-Unity honored nation-builders
- Those that died in a manner consistent with their age
- Those that died for a righteous war for their nation
- Those that parented children (biological/spiritual)
- Those that embodied the morals that we aspire to

THE SAGES

I can hardly account for the amount of times that I've stood in a libation circle or performed libations and when it came time to allow the attending audience to offer their verbal libations; how many deceased actors and entertainers names are delivered (Michael Jackson, Notorious BIG, Aaliyah, Left Eye, KWK...). I deduce that this is an issue indicative of a lack of study and awareness of who OUR Kemunity warrior scholars truly are.

I would advise the reader to be discerning when giving honor to Ancestral spirits and be very mindful about what type of spirits you strive to invoke...within and without.

I make a ritualistic practice of not only praying to my Egun/Lidlotis/Nananom Nsamanfo but, of also praying **FOR** my Egun/Lidlotis/Nananom Nsamanfo. I pray that they continue to evolve and learn in Orun. In our Afrakan tradition reincarnation is a central theme to our acknowledgment of karmic influences on our lives. We recognize that our children are our ancestors who return in order to serve a purpose for the season and most often to complete an unfinished work. Some call this our past life mission or karmic imprint.

Who are your Egun?

Those who are of your blood lineage.
Elijah Muhammad, Huey Newton, Patrice Lumumba, Steven Biko, Halle Selassie, Araminta Ross (Harriet Tubman), and Queen Hapshetsut are not everyone's personal Egun. They are OUR national Egun and can be invoked during communal ceremonies but, they are not *your* Egun.

Some state that the "**Egungun**" are the collective Ancestral body and together they represent a single Spiritual Force, which is considered an Orisa.

Your Egun don't have to be those who practiced Traditional Afrakan Spiritual Systems, either. They are still developing in Orun and still need light.

For example:

My family contains a large number of people who are from the Muscogee Nation and the Caribbean. I address them at my family Aforemuka collectively.

Prior to getting into any really heavy exchange, I took 10 days and taught them my basic Yoruba invocations.

I would say the phrase in Yoruba and then provide the English translation.

Now, this is not truly necessary because, Esu, the divine messenger translates all languages for us but, it was my way of honoring my Egun and giving them a language that we could exchange with that held a much more powerful vibration than English. Plus, knowing that it was something we were both stripped of (our native language) it made me feel good to assist them in reversing the enslavement process however I could for them.

Your Egun determine who is also your Egun, not you. This is where learning a divination system can be quite helpful. You can cast OBI to question your Egun as to who should be represented on the Ancestral Aforemuka.

Some deceased family members may not have choosen to do *any* spiritual work to elevate their spirits, which is essential to their continued development when they return to Aye. Work with those who work with you.

THE SAGES

Sangoma

I am particularly partial to the Sangoma tradition of the Bantu and the process of Ancestral veneration and channeling that's used to service their supporting villages. In this wonderful tradition the Sangoma go through a rigorous process by the name of Kutfwasa as a part of their initiation into the order of Sangoma. Working with the ancestral spirits is regarded as high honor. It is stated that all people have "Lidlotis" (Ancestors), but all don't have the ability to communicate with them in a way that is lucid.

The terms we're using are Bantu in origin as Zulu/Xhosa is a Bantu language.

Traditionally in some Sangoma traditions, Sangoma work with paternal Lidlotis, maternal Lidlotis, and the collective Lidlotis spirits.

When the Zulu talk about "Lidlotis", they are speaking of "deceased" family, spiritual guardians, nature spirits and universal energies.

Sangoma work in huts called "Ndumba"; where the Ancestors reside. Sangoma work with Lidlotis and allow the Lidlotis to continue to live their lives vicariously through them.

Sangoma summon the ancestors by inhaling certain plants, dancing, chanting, and drumming.

Sangoma access the guidance of Lidlotis via:

- Ancestral spirit possession
- Channeling Ancestral spirits
- Throwing Bones
- Dream Interpretation

THE SAGES

Establishing your Gateway

THE GATEWAY

Establishing your gateway -

Jingili - Gulimancema term from West Afraka translated in English as "Altar"

Aforemuka - (pronounced: Ah four-ray Moo-kah) is a Twi word translated in English as "Altar"

Tambiko - Ki-Bantu term translated in English as "libation".

From here on we will utilize these Afrakan terms.

A Jingili is your personal spiritual focal point. In this segment I'll provide some foundational techniques for establishing your portal but, do not be afraid to intuit what your guiding spirits would like to use in order to establish the two way communication that you aspire to have with them. Once you develop some proficiency with the divination techniques outlined in this book, you'll be able to even query the entities that you're honoring through your Jingili as to what they'd like to experience at your sacred space.

An Aforemuka can be placed on a table or on the floor. I would suggest you start on the floor and once divination proficiency is achieved you can question your Ancestors as to if they'd like to be elsewhere.

Grasping the Root of Divine Power   55

These are items I recommended to collect for your Jingili:

- **Water** - Water serves as a spiritual receptacle and can be used to scry into; for water meditations. Water serves as a representation of one of the 4 major earth elements.
- **Candle(s)** - The Candle flame serves as a "lighthouse" for the spirits that we are beckoning to commune with us. Spirits are attracted to flame. Also, candles are wonderful for scrying into to focus your intentions through fire meditations. Candles can be used for prayer rituals. They also allow us to represent one of the 4 major earth elements (fire).
- **Plants** - This signifies the resting place of the Ara (body) of our Ancestors and is a representation of life as well as one of the 4 major earth elements (earth).
- **Pictures** - Paternal/Maternal Egun/Lidlotis/Nananom Nsamanfo male and female should be portrayed. Photographs and images assist in focusing our attention and are a way of honoring those who lived and died in order to make space on the planet for our arrival.

Caution: Do not place any pictures of living relatives on your Jingili. This could quicken them to the Ancestral realm.

- **Incense** - This is used to clear the space of malevolent energy and to stimulate spiritual communication/mind-set. I'd recommend Frankincense, Myrrh, Sandalwood and even burning powered herbs that were favorites of the Egun who are on the Altar (Cinnamon, Curry, Basil, Rue, KWK....).
- **White Cloth or wooden Mat** - A wooden mat serves well for Aforemukas placed on floors

All items should be cleansed with sea saltwater and smudged

THE GATEWAY

I'm also partial to Jingili that incorporate articles that were used by your Ancestors (perfumes, bracelets, charms, smoking pipes).

Crystals are also a great addition for your Aforemuka.

You can write a list of desires and goals and place them on your Jingili but, I'd suggest you turn them text side down in the event that your Aforemuka is exposed to public observation/scrutiny. If your desires and goals are your own you should hold them close to your heart in a sacred/secret way.

** A friend of mine needed to establish an Aforemuka in her home but, was concerned about her family members who resided with her who saw this method of spiritual expression as "spooky" and sinister. I created a movable/concealable Jingili for her out of a kitchen cabinet. I laid the cabinet length-wise on its side and installed two small luggage padlocks on the side of the cabinets. She was able to install all of her spiritual paraphernalia inside of the cabinet and using the open cabinet door as additional space. This allowed her to perform all of the needed Jingili work and meditation and when finished close it, fasten the locks ,and cover it with a piece of fabric. This was a perfectly acceptable/appreciated solution.

Once we've gathered our materials it's essential that we cleanse the space that we'll be using to establish our sacred portal. **Take a moment to note that this Jingili is not to double as anything other than what it's been created for.** That means do not allow your guest to leave their drinks, keys, umbrella's, plates of beans and rice, bottles of Henrock or EZ Jezus, bootleg DVD's, mail, or anything else on it.

Cleansing your space -

Spiritual cleanses are an important part of divination. It clears the vision and makes us more attractive to benevolent spirits.

1st - cleanse yourself.

Take a bath or shower ,first, to remove the physical dirt from your body; I recommend using Black soap for this purpose. Once that's completed, proceed with the spiritual cleanse.

You can perform a simple spiritual cleanse using:

White Rose Petals
Florida Water or Rose Water
Sea Salt
Spring Water
*Also see the section "So Fresh and So Clean Clean" for more baths

Mix the ingredients of the bath in a large natural container. Light a white candle.

Take the contents and pour them over your entire body from the crown of your head downward.
While doing this, visualize the spiritual sludge loosening its grip on your body and falling to your wayside and down the shower drain.
Some baths you do not rinse off. This one you will as its purpose is to remove harmful energy.

*You can take this same bath mixture and sprinkle it on the floor of the room that will house your Aforemuka.

THE GATEWAY

Once you've removed any harmful energy from yourself it's now time to consecrate the space for your Jingili. Walk throughout your space and get a feel for where your Egun may want to be; perhaps facing a window to the East where they can view their home, or on a sunny back porch where there is plenty of fresh air and plant life, maybe the family room where they can be at the center of family activity.

I would strongly advise against placing the Aforemuka anywhere sexual intercourse may occur. Sex in front of an Aforemuka will "heat" things up in a way that could be exploited by watchful spirit energies and misinterpreted as an intentional ritualistic procedure; in fact sex *is* a ritual...every time. It's not that sex is an impure act but, it is a powerful act that can direct the energy of a space or unified intention with great Ase behind it. If you perform this act in front of an Aforemuka without proper preparation and incantation you're putting your head into the proverbial lion's mouth.

If you have to set your Jingili up in your bedroom, use a white sheet or wardrobe divider to separate the spaces. A closet can even be used as long as that closet is dedicated, solely to that purpose.

In order to clean the space I'd suggest you first do a thorough cleanse with a pine cleaner (see "So Fresh and so Clean Clean" for this). Clean the floors, walls, furniture, and underneath your home furnishings, as well. While doing this open a window in order to provide an escape route for energies that are being expelled from the home.

Smudging

Smudging is a process of "smoking" the space out with an incense or smoky substance. Malevolent spirits do not like smoke and will make their exodus in the presence of it. To smudge, sage is a great plant that can be used and can be found in natural food markets, "Botanicas", and can even be grown.

You can even go outdoors and use dried tree leaves or dried herbs to smudge with. As always, let your ORI direct you.

Frankincense is quite effective for this purpose.

As the smudge substance burns pray/speak/meditate over it asking your Egun/Lidlotis/Nananom Nsamanfo to remove any malevolent energy from your home and usher in energy that is healthy for your welfare and development.

After we smudge, we are now ready to assemble our Jingili.

If possible I would suggest cleaning and smudging your entire home before establishing your space. This is not an instant process and may require a few days of work and preparation but, it is well worth it.

―――――――――――――――――――――――

During the construction of the Aforemuka wear clothing that represents the strongest vibration of Ancestral veneration possible. I would suggest Afrakan peace-drobe/attire. You can even wrap a white piece of fabric about you or for men; a white piece of fabric can be tied at the waist.

OUR Egun/ enjoy aligning with us, more, when we dress in the patterns and motifs that honor them.

Now, it's time to bring together the pieces of our Jingili.

Everything should be cleansed in a sea saltwater solution and smoked/smudged thoroughly. You can also wipe them down with an essential oil.

Again a Jingili can reside on a table or on the floor. I, personally, suggest the floor as the Egun like to be close to the ground. In some traditions Egun shrines are even placed in bathrooms or in places in the home where there are pipes that lead into the ground.

Let your own ORI/Egun guide you to what is most correct for you/them.

Most will tell you to use a clean white cloth for your shrine. This is a good starter point for your shrine as white gives the Egun/Lidlotis/Nananom Nsamanfo a "cool" space to convene. It also represents purity and new beginnings. Many of OUR Egungun have died horrendous deaths and were not given proper entombment rites so, whenever possible we want to invite them into the most sacred and purest environments that we can produce.

Feel your way through the placement of objects on your Aforemuka as you will instinctively arrange the items in a way that allows you to maximize its power as a spiritual/cerebral focal point.

I would also suggest not placing anything synthetic on your Jingili, if it can be avoided. I typically use only organic substances. So, my pictures are framed in metal or wood, water is kept in glasses or calabash, food is served on earthenware or wooden bowls, KWK…

Once your objects are arranged on your Aforemuka it's time to call your Egun/Lidlotis/Nananom Nsamanfo to the sacred space.

1. 1st Light your candle on your Aforemuka.

The amount of Candles you place on your Jingili can vary as some will place one candle for every Egun represented or others will place 7 candles and 7 glasses of water for the 7 major religions. I suggest, for now, you start with one white candle and one glass of water. Make sure all stickers are removed from the candle if it is in a glass shute and it's been washed with salt water.

2. "**Tambiko**" is a Ki-Bantu word translated into English as "Libation". This step is crucial in the process of reconnecting with OUR Afrakan source and grasping the root of OUR collective divine power. We should use OUR Afrakan names for OUR high order deities and Egun/Lidlotis/Nananom Nsamanfo. In doing this we are able to pull from the eternal spiritual pool of the original beings of this world and the next. There is no need to de-emphasize the importance of calling OUR revered spirits by their proper name. Remember the title of this series is "**How to be an Afrakan**". For a de-cultured oppressed people this concept can be bloodcurdling. The culturally retarded have been trained that it's best that we warehouse the culture of OUR ethnic origins in closets, shadows, musty basements and strive to be as inclusive as we possibly can. When pouring Tambiko, innerstand you are inviting *your* Nananom Nsamanfo/Egungun/Lidlotis to you.

Do not be ashamed of your lineage. Align with your Nananom Nsamanfo/Egungun/Lidlotis, and they'll align with you. No people show shame of their origins like dispossessed Africans. No Rabbi, Iman, Pastor, or any other professor of religion compromises for you; there is no need to do it for them or their followers. It is treasonous to your culture and Ancestors.

THE GATEWAY

Pour your spring water into your receptacles that you've placed on your Jingili.

Take that same water; dip your middle and ring finger of your right hand into it and sprinkle the water about your sacred space and Jingili reciting **Adura 1** and **Adura 2** from the "**Initiating the dialogue**" section of this book.

You are now ready to meditate at your Aforemuka or recite words that invoke the blessings and protection of your Egun.

I would suggest your service and maintain your Jingili daily.

The water that you put in your receptacles can be allowed to evaporate. I see this as the Egun getting their full drink.

You can also use this space to appropriate meals to your Egun/Lidlotis/Nananom Nsamanfo and present your Adimu (Offerings).

If you put flowers on your Aforemuka, make sure they are changed out when they wither.

*Tip – *I like to take the shrunken dried flower petals of my Jingili flower arrangements and use them later for smudging. Remember everything that sits in this consecrated space is charged with Ase. Recycle when/where you can! This honors the divine.*

Optional Aforemuka paraphernalia:

Skulls – Represent the temporal nature of the life journey and our connection to our Egun/Lidlotis/Nananom Nsamanfo.

Rum - Loosens the tongue and eases the mental grip that sometimes can prevent spiritual fluidity. Rum is also a drink of celebration.

Jewelry - It's good to leave your body adornments on your Jingili in order to charge them with the Ase of that consecrated space prior to wearing them.

Books - Books retain and project the power of their words. By putting them on your Aforemuka you amplify the potency of the messages they convey. Use books that hold special transforming meaning to you.

Flowers - Spirits love flowers.

Fruit- This represents the fruitful harvest that the spirits have always provided for you and will continue to provide.

Dolls - These are focal points that are infused with the energy of your Egun/Lidlotis/Nananom Nsamanfo. They should be treated as living beings....because they are.

Aumba – The Aumba is also known as the Opa Egun or Igi Egun. This is a wooden staff/branch which is used to call the Egun forth as well as to banish harmful energy.

The Aumba is used to assist in summoning your Egun by tapping it on the floor before your Jingili.

*I would suggest consulting with an Elder to have an Igi Egun properly consecrated and fed for your use. Depending on the circumstances different types of Opa Egun are required.

THE GATEWAY

Initiating the dialogue

INITIATING THE DIALOGUE

Initiating the Dialogue -

The act of exchanging ideas or concerns between your spirit self and members of the larger spirit consciousness should not be taken lightly but, also should not invoke feelings of fear or inadequacy.

Many people claim that they do not know how to "pray" or what to say, even. This type of fear comes as a result of an aggressive western campaign to monopolize, even commercialize, spirit relationship and the process of individuals gaining personalized clarity of sight of their own spirit shape and privilege.

In truth we are engaged in dialogue with the spirit realm during every moment of our existence. In light of that, conversations should deliberately be guided and directed to the proper spirit entities depending on the energy being addressed. There is no need to invoke an artificial character or persona when talking to spirit guardians. Keep it real.

Observe that Afrakans are a people of rhythm and rhyme. Emotions move spirits to action and even give birth to spirit entities. Poetry is the vehicle of all Afrakan exchange. From the Griots, to the backwoods spiritualist, to the "Last Poets", to the Emcees who move the crowd; no one puts down or sends up lyrical word power like an authentic Afrakan traversing the river of spiritual flow and cadence.

Don't be afraid to scribe your own prayers; *I recommend that you do*. Write a poem that you can recite to the spirits. They are moved by poetry.

Language-

As an Afrakan, I am inclined to recite my incantations, praise names, and invocations in the tongue of my Egun/Lidlotis/Nananom Nsamanfo...out Loud (there is power in wind exhaled from speaking). The tone and rhythm of Afrakan language sends out a powerfully high vibratory impulse. Since early european invasion, and even up until this day, there has been a hostile mission to eradicate the Afrikan continent of its native languages and the true pronunciation of native terms (removal of hard consonants, clicks, and tonal expressions). The languages of melaninated people are the languages of divinity; spoken consistently, it begins to cure and reverse the Maafan process.

Language provides the framework for the perceptual experience of life as it confirms and seals the agreement of corporeal reality. While Afrakans are steadily being stripped of their traditional tongue the perpetrators of this crime and the proponents of the universalizing beast language, English, are studying and archiving the vibratory tones of traditional Afrakan speech for their use.

Beastly speech keeps us within the lower fields of awareness. Why do I keep referring to this English tongue as being beastly? The mark of the beast as referred to in Christian mythology is not a physical tattoo of "666" but, it is the language that sits in the frontal lobe region of the brain (frontal lobe is located at the forehead location). This language is English. This is the language that all need in order to buy and sell throughout the "civilized" world. The scope of this book is not broad enough for me to continue to expound on this truth but, in order to transcend to the higher realms of metaphysical reality and corporal reality construction proper selection of language is indispensable.

INITIATING THE DIALOGUE

Adura 1:
Properly recognizing the forces in nature that conspire to sustain the life process that we all are a part of is a critically polite thing to do. For those trapped in the confusing labyrinth of the English language there is little to no code for proper social recognition embedded in this language context. For instance English speakers say, "Hi"; this greeting can apply to a 7, 17, or 70 year old. Western culture provides few means to show homage and RAspect through language sub-context.

This is not Black Power.

This is cultural socio-suicidal. For those seeking to connect with a healthier way of being must learn to greet the universe and all of its inhabitants showing the proper reverence and acknowledgement for the roles that each element/person plays in the cosmic cooperative. The next Adura is a template that you can use to show reverence to the seen and unseen forces of OUR existence. It can be used during the Tambiko process, when greeting the dawning, or even when preparing to communicate with your Egun.

Say:

Mo júbà Olódùmarè, Oba a té rere k' áyé

I revere the Creator, The Creator who governs the universe

Mo júbà àtiyo ojó

I revere the sunrise

Mo júbà àtiwò oòrùn

I revere the sunset

Mo júbà ilè ògééré a f' okó ye' rí

I revere Mama Earth

Mo júbà Òrúnmìlà Elérìí Ìpín

I revere Òrúnmìlà, witness to Creation

Mo júbà igba Irúnmolè ojùkòtùn
I revere the 200 deity on the right hand side of the Creator

Mo júbà igba Irúnmolè ojùkòsìn
I revere the 200 deity on the left hand side of the Creator

Mo júbà òkànlé-ní Irinwó Irúnmolè
I revere the 401 dwellers of orun, the primordial beings

Mo júbà Akódá
I revere Òrúnmìlà's first student Akódá

Mo júbà Asèdá
I revere Akódá's first student Asèdá

Mo júbà Àràbà lótù Ifè
I revere the worldwide head of Babaláwo and Orisa worshippers

Mo júbà àwon Ìyá, afín'jú eye
I revere the Mothers, The beautiful Birds

Mo júbà Egúngún Ilé
I revere the collective Ancestral Lineage (Names can be said)

Mo júbà Bàbá
I revere my father

Mo júbà Yèyé
I revere my mother

Mo júbà Olúwo
I revere my earthly spiritual guide and spiritual parents

Mo júbà Ojùgbònà
I revere my spiritual parents who clear the way for me

Mo júbà àwon Alàsekù
I revere those who have completed sacred rites, before me

Ase Ase Ase O
May it be so

*"Mo júbà" can be replaced with "Ìjúbà" if said in/for a group

INITIATING THE DIALOGUE

Adura 2:

One of the most important tenants in Afrakan attitude is the ability to function with superconcious mastery over your animal and humanistic nature. This concept is indicated by the Kemetic "NEB HU". This structure reminds us that our waistline serves as the divider between the "HRU" and the "SET" regions in our own physical being and our life should be one that reflects the balance between our own upper and lower regions. In order to do this, the fiery disposition of our lower nature or lower order thinking must be tempered with the cool headedness of our upper/HRU (heaven) nature as reflected by a cool head. To be cool, calm, and rational in our dealings brings fortune. This Adura extends this wish and charge to our spirit world.

Omi tutu
May the water be cool and refreshed
Ona tutu
May our road and path be cool and refreshed
Ile tutu
May our home/house be cool and refreshed
Tutu Laroye
Refresh Esu the Messenger
Tutu Ori
May our own inner deity be refreshed and cooled
Tutu Emi
May the spirit of divine breath be refreshed and cooled
Tutu Babanla, Tutu Iyanla
May the Ancestors be refreshed
Ase Ase Ase O!
May it be so

Grasping the Root of Divine Power

Adura 3:

We are a hand-selected fraction of the supreme being augmenting our spiritual form in order to participate in this earthly sensory journey. ORI is your divine flame born from Oludumare's spark of life; always connected to Oludumare's celestial lungful of air that is everywhere and now-here. ORI is the ONLY Orisa that will walk with you from beginning to end regardless of what tribute you offer.

Strengthen your ORI and rise up as the marvelous work of creativity that you are.

Ori san mi, Ori san mi, Ori san mi
Ori guide me, Ori guide me, Ori guide me
Ori san igede, Ori san igede, Ori san igede
Ori support me, Ori support me, Ori support me
Ori oto san mi ki nni owo lowo
Ori support my abundance
Ori tan san mi ki nbimo le mio
Ori support my future children
Ori oto san mi ki nni aya
Ori support my relationship
Ori oto san mi ki nkole mole
Ori protect my house
Ori ni ma sin, Ori ni ma sin, Ori ni ma sin
It is my Ori whom I shall worship, it is my Ori whom I shall worship, it is my Ori whom I shall worship
Oloma ajiki, iwa' ni mope
Protector of the children, my inner character is thankful
Ase
May it be so

INITIATING THE DIALOGUE

Adura 4:

Yoruba adura to greet the dawning:

Olódùmarè àwa omo rẹ dé,
Olodumare we, the children, have come
Adé láti wá gba ìre tiwa,
We have come to get our blessings for today
Asìn ńbè ọ lórúkọ odù mérìndínlógún
We are begging you in the name of all the 16 major odu
Kí o gbó ìre tòní yí
That you should listen to the prayer of the day
Bí o bá gbọ kí o múu ṣẹ,
When you hear our prayer, please grant our request
Kí o máa ṣọ Baba wa
Protect our Fathers
Kí o máa ṣọ Ìyá wa
Protect our Mothers
Kí o máa ṣọ Aya/Ọkọ wa
Protect our Wives/Husbands
Kí o máa ṣọ Ọmọ wa,
Protect our Children
Kí o máa ṣọ Alábàá gbélé àti òré wa
Protect our Neighbors and Friends
Títí tófi mó ibi tí aní ẹni dé
And extend your protection to all our well-wishers
Pàápàá àti àwọn mòlébí wa
Most especially our relatives
Afi ọlójó òní bè ó
We beg you in the name of the Orisa that rules today

Kí o fi yè dénú
For you to be mindful of what we are doing
Kí o fi yè dékùn
For you to be mindful of all our proceedings
Kí o fi yè dé gbogbo ara
For you to be mindful of all our generalities
Bàbá awa Ọmọ rẹ là ń pè ó
Father, we the children are calling upon you
Èlà ìború Èlà bòyè Èlà boṣíṣe
Èlà ìború Èlà bòyè Èlà boṣíṣe

Adura 5 -

Oriki to the Egun/Ancestors

Egungun kiki egungun.
Praise the Ancestors.
Egun iku ranran fe awo ku opipi.
Ancestors who have preserved the mysteries of featherless flight.
O da so bo fun le wo.
You create words of reverence and power.
Egun iku bata bango egun de.
On the strong mat you spread your power.
Bi aba f'atori na le egun a se de.
The Ancestors are here.
Ase.
May it be so.

INITIATING THE DIALOGUE

OBI
The keeper of the sacred truth

OBI - KEEPER OF THE SACRED TRUTH

The keeper of the sacred truth

The Obi oracle can reveal a myriad of answers and perspectives while assisting in every area of our lives but, the oracle is ultimately charged and triangulated using your own Ase (Power, vigor, electromagnetic energy).

Many will tell you that the Obi has only 5 basic positions, or 9, or 16, or 256...all of these answers are true but, what I've found is the OBI positions and answers are limited or expanded by your ability to see the often times subtle hints and clues that the oracle affords the diviner. There are times when you'll cast your OBI and the position, as commonly taught, should mean one thing but, in fact, is saying something totally different to you. Go with your intuition. Your OBI will talk to you in a language that you innerstand as they are infused with your own energy.

In fact all things in existence are talking to you. There are messages and latent communication that inhabit all things manifested on the planet. Every rock, mineral, plant, animal, force of nature..... EVERYthing is a force in and of itself. All things are alive and have a bond with the frequently "unseen" world that exists concurrent with the "seen" world.

So when one ask, "Is OBI divination accurate?". A reasonable response would be that OBI divination or any divination is as effective as an individual's ability to tune into the universal voice and pulse that resonates in all things. Some use OBI, cowries, cigar ash, tea leaves, fire, palms, eyes, cards, KWK...

The oracle that will be most precise for you will be the one you find most intuitive.

For example:

There may be systems that exist on another side of the globe from you using a language that is foreign to you. For you this may not be the most accurate oracle if you're unable to speak the language that the tools of that oracle speak through. As you begin to cast more you'll hear the voice in all things. You'll even begin to see "cast patterns" appear across people and situations. You'll know that all things are a pattern. If you're knowledge is I-Ching, then you'll see I-Ching patterns in all things but, if they're OBI, you'll see OBI cast appear in your head as you meditate or even as you encounter people for the first time. Soon the tools will become less important than your ability to intuit and connect. The tools provide details and focus but, just know that you are triangulating energy between the oracle (OBI), yourself, and the spirit that you are asking questions to.

Many faces of the OBI

'Bese saka' means a bunch or sack of cola nuts, a widely-used crop for the economy of Ghana and a favorite of the northern tribes. Metaphorically, the symbol relates to affluence and wealth, prosperity and plenteousness, camaraderie and synthesis through the extended idea that agriculture and trade bring people together.

Yoruba Pataki-

Obi was well loved and respected by Olofi, because he had a pure and sincere heart. To award his good deeds, Olofi made him white and shiny and placed him at the top of the highest palm tree, so everyone could see him from afar.

As soon as Obi saw himself in such high position, he turned vain and arrogant. Obi asked Esu, who was one of his closest friends, to invite all of Esu's friends to a party that he was preparing. Esu, who could see how much he had changed, invited all the beggars, homeless and poor people he could find.

When Obi saw his beautiful and spotless house filled with all those dirty, smelly, ragged beggars, he almost had a heart attack and pulled them all out, yelling. The guests left the house and so did Esu.

A few days later, Olofi asked Esu, who is the divine messenger, to take a message to Obi, and Esu refused. When Olofi asked why, Esu told him the story of the party; filled with sadness, Olofi dressed up as a beggar and went to knock at OBI's door. When Obi opened the door and saw the beggar, he told him to leave his home and slammed the door on Olofi's face. Olofi walked away a few steps and called Obi out loud, saying:

- Obi Meye Lori Emi Ofe!!!!
Which means:
- Obi, see who I really am!!!!!

When Obi saw the beggar was Olofi, he got really scared, and trembling from head to toes asked forgiveness from Olofi.

Olofi forgave him, but as a reminder of his arrogance he was condemned: he would stay white and sweet inside, symbolizing his previous state; he would have a dark hard cover, to remind him of his transgression, and he would have another green cover that would mean the hope that he could learn from his mistake and become pure and honorable again. By falling from his tree and rolling in dirt until someone would pick him up, he would always be reminded of the poor he would not accept by becoming one of them; and by turning into the Obi oracle he would serve Esu forever, the only friend that wanted to show him the truth about his vanity, and always be the messenger of the voice of the Orisas.

When referring to OBI it can get a bit confusing as there are three different oracle tools that are possibly referenced when one says the word "Obi" :

- Kola nut
- Coconut
- Cowrie Shell with Coconut Backing

We're going to begin with the Kola nut

MANY FACES OF THE OBI

84 HRU Assaan-Anu

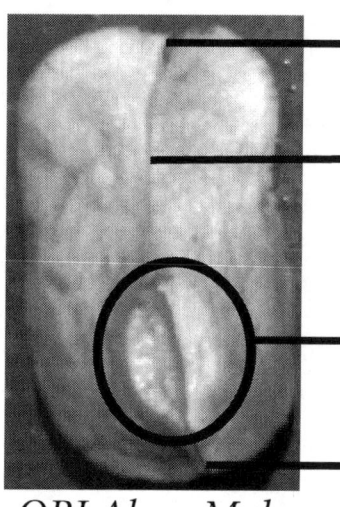

"Head" of the OBI Segment

This straight line going up the middle of the OBI signifies that this is a "male" OBI segment

Kola nut "Heart" removed.

"Tail" of the Obi

OBI Ako - Male Kola nut Pointing "UP"

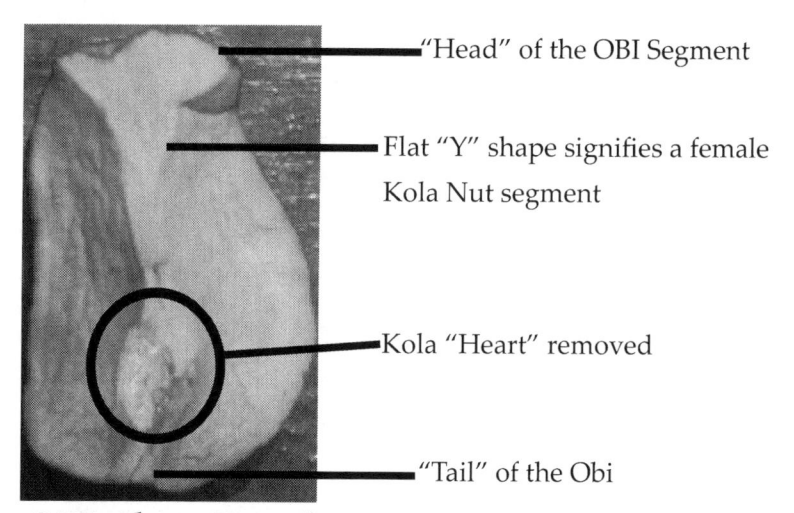

"Head" of the OBI Segment

Flat "Y" shape signifies a female Kola Nut segment

Kola "Heart" removed

"Tail" of the Obi

OBI Abo - Female Kola nut Pointing "UP"

Grasping the Root of Divine Power

Kola nut

Kola nut is a nut native to Afraka ranging in color from white to dark red.

For the purpose of divination we use Obi Abata; also known as 'Iya Obi' (The Mother Obi),as opposed to OBI Gbanja (2 lobes). Lobes are segments that comprise the nut in its entirety. We also call these lobes segments.

This sacred nut is also, often, used as Adimu to Orisa and Egun.

The male Obi segments, also known as Ako Obi.
The female Obi segments, also known as Abo Obi

Typically you'll be casting with 4 lobe OBI Abata though Abata commonly have 3-6 lobes.

When selecting your OBI pay careful attention to its freshness. Do not use Kola with lobes that are beginning to separate from one another. This means that they are drying out and losing their freshness. Make sure there is no mold on them or any other physical damage.

Medicinal uses:
Kola nuts are often used to treat whooping cough, and asthma. Their also used as an aphrodisiac, stimulant, cardio-tonic, bronchodilator, alkaloid, for theo-bromine, laxative, heart stimulants and sedative.
Dry kola nut is used for producing Kola nut beverages, liquor, and confectioneries.

MANY FACES OF THE OBI

Opening the world of the OBI Abata

The whole Obi Abata must be split into its four lobes before one can divine with it. Never use a knife or any other metal object to split your OBI. Your OBI will be infused with your Ase and by introducing foreign implements you could disturb the energy relationship between you and the oracle.

If the kola nut is particularly fresh the segments may be tricky to divide. If this is the case with your OBI, you may apply a little force and roll the Obi Abata between your thumb and forefinger; this will slowly release the segments and make it easier to open the OBI.

If you damage the Kola Nut in the process of separating its lobes; apologize to it and place them to the side. You cannot use these for divination or offering. Select another Kola nut.

You can use your OBI set for as long as the spirits you cast to say it's OK. Some people use a new set of Kola each time they cast; depending on where you live this may not be practical for you. You can set your OBI in a bowl of cool water, in a cool place, and this will help to preserve their freshness. I prefer this method as the OBI will then build Ase along with you over "time".

Before casting with kola always remove the heart and offer them to the spirit you are casting to. The heart will be at the tail and will be the reddest part of the Kola (See illustration on page 84).

The OBI opens the secrets of the universe to the diviner -

The Kola nut is the original OBI oracle and when accessible, I suggest you use it to cast with. You'll sense the energy in this oracle the moment you see it land on your casting surface.

The OBI, with its 2 Ako segments and its 2 Abo segments, reminds of us the cooperative relationship that must always exist between male and female energies in the inner/outer-verse. The OBI Abata is referred to as "Iya OBI" because it is the 4 lobe configuration that brings the potentiality of creation into the physical world. The 2 male segments and 2 female segments instruct us that sexual balance opens the gateways to the invisible dominion… where/when supremacy initiates.

When it's time to replace your OBI with another set you can question the OBI as to how it would like to be returned to its essence. It may want to be presented as an offering to your ORI or to your Egun, or it may want to be left near a stream, rock, crossroad intersection, or tree. Cast asking for where OBI would like to be placed after usage.

If you use a fresh Obi and plan on replacing it after one divination session; you can ask if it is permissible to consume the OBI. This will bring you fortune.

Do not permit anyone else to handle your Obi or any of your divination tools, for that matter.
Treasure this sacred Oracle. The OBI is an Orisa. Never forget this.

MANY FACES OF THE OBI

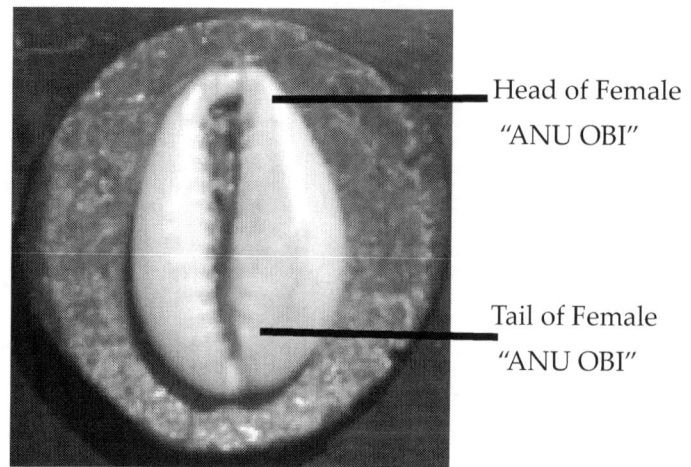

"ANU OBI" - *Female Pointing "UP"*

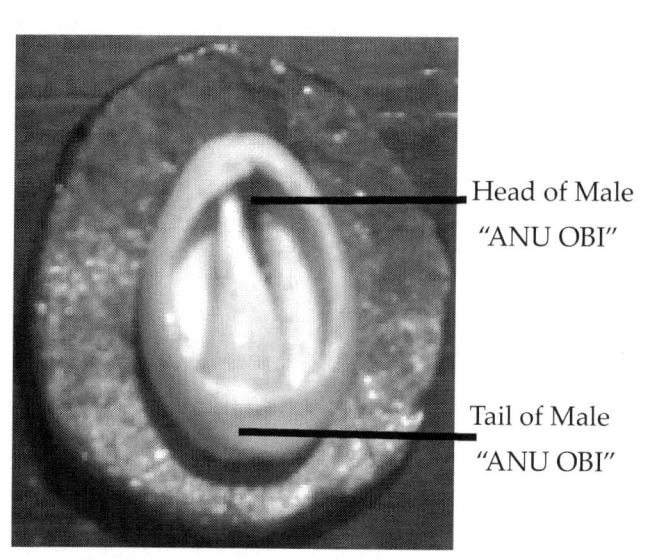

"ANU OBI" - *Male Pointing "UP"*

"ANU OBI"

In the picture to the left we see examples of two Open segments.

As with the Kola nut we are able to divine using male and female segments with head/tail orientation; as well as light/dark calculations.

This form of OBI oracle was created as a result of OUR tradition traveling across the Atlantic recorded through the psyche/blood of enslaved Afrakans. These tireless spiritual warriors saw that in this region of the globe their sacred Kola nut oracle was no longer accessible to them so, being the "solutionaries" that Afrakans traditionally are they fashioned a new OBI oracle to cast with.

This OBI type is made from the hard outer shell of the coconut and cut cowry shells.

This "ANU OBI" alternate is a greatly respected form of the oracle used by many Orisa priest/priestesses and is often favored because it allows a person to purchase a set once and not continue to be accountable for Kola nut purchases.

As with Kola nut you should develop an Ase exchange bond with your Anu OBI set. Keep them in a sanctified place. I prefer to keep my "ANU OBI" on my Aforemuka but, they can also be kept in a white cloth bag or a wrapped in silk material.

◇◇◇◇◇◇◇◇◇◇◇◇◇◇◇◇◇◇◇◇◇◇◇◇◇◇◇◇◇◇◇◇◇◇

Let's move forward with the cocnut OBI oracle as this is where you will begin your casting studies........

MANY FACES OF THE OBI

Medicinal uses for the OBI/Coconut:

- Coconuts are a power food. They have robust quantities of B1, B2, B3, C, Calcium, Iodine, Magnesium, Potassium, Phosphorus, and iron.
- Coconuts serve as an excellent intestinal cleanser, digestive agent, and are good for ulcers and constipation.
- The oil from the coconut can be used for cuts, burns, to maintain healthy hair and skin, as an excellent laxative, and is great to prepare food with.
- Coconut milk can be used to feed infant children when the mother is unable to breast feed.
- The water of coconut has been known to cure the urinal disorder Dieresis and alleviate the affects of anemia.
- Coconut water is rich in electrolytes; making it the perfect sports drink.
- Coconut water mixed with gin is a cure for the vaginal disorder leucorrhea.
- The green skin of the coconut can be boiled and made into a tea which is good to tone and purify the blood.
- The white coconut "meat" can be eaten in the dawning to remove stomach worms.

Coconuts can provide the majority of what a person needs for nourishment. There have been survivor stories where individuals have reported living solely from the water and flesh of coconuts for up to 6 months!

Preparing the coconut:

In selecting the coconut it's important that you pick one that has a healthy appearance and is full of coconut water.

Pick the coconut that has an energy that resonates with you; as opposed to just grabbing one from the top of the heap.

Once you've obtained *your* coconut you must now split the hard outer shell to expose the coconut "meat".

In order to do this use a hammer or a rock outside of your home.

Do not throw the coconut against the floor in order to break it open. This is considered a violation of this sacred oracle.

I find it easier to strike the coconut in a straight-line across its center while pushing it towards the hammer and slowly turning it until I'm back at my original position. This usually allows me to save the most coconut water and leave the majority of the coconut whole.

Save the coconut water in a white ceramic or glass bowl.

Break the coconut pieces (white "meat") off with your hand (you'll need 4) you can shape these pieces however you like. Some prefer square others triangular. Over time you'll discover a shape that speaks to you most.

Do not use any utensils other than your own hand to break and shape the coconut pieces. Using a knife or other implement could disturb the Ase of the oracle and the energy bond that you are now beginning to establish with it.

MANY FACES OF THE OBI

At this point I like to either have a piece of material or small calabash bowl to place the OBI in. I'd recommend you handle the OBI as if they were the last seeds of nourishment on a dying planet.

Light a white candle either at your Aforemuka or near to your casting surface.
Recite **Adura 1** and **Adura 2** from **"Initiating the Dialogue"** while offering Tambiko.
Break 9 small pieces of obi from each of your 4 OBI segments. Sprinkle these on your Jingili.
Next, mix 8 ounces of spring water (do not use mineral or distilled water as they are devoid of life) with the coconut water you saved earlier in the procedure.
You will then sprinkle the mixture over your obi and chant the following:

Ago Obi, Ago Obi, Ago Obi
Listen Obi
Obi ni ibi iku
The obi averts death
Obi ni ibi arun
The obi averts sickness
Obi ni ibi ofo
The obi averts loss
Obi ni ibi fitibo
The obi averts being overwhelmed
Obi ni ibi idina
The obi averts obstacles

Now hold all four obi in your left hand and touch ground/floor three times and chant:

Ile mo ki e o
Ile mo ki e o
Ile mo ki e o
(Shrine, I greet you)

Switch hands then chant:

Ile mo ki e o iki eye
Ile mo ki e o iki eye
Ile mo ki e o iki eye
(Shrine, I greet you with honor)

Switch back to left again and with right hand touch floor/ground and chant:

Obi Egungun ile mo ki e o iki eye
Obi Egungun ile mo ki e o iki eye
Obi Egungun ile mo ki e o iki eye
(Obi, My Ancestor I greet you with honor)

While gently shaking the obi in the palm of your hands clasped together; chant:

Akinmoran, Akinmoran, Akinmoran!
(May the forces in heavan assist the diviner on earth)

Blow three times on the obi in your hands, ask your question and "throw" them to your casting surface.

MANY FACES OF THE OBI

5 *the Hard Way*

5 THE HARD WAY

5 Position OBI -

We now have a rudimentary innerstanding of the masculine and feminine forces and how they work within the cradle of darkness and the vehicle of light.

Now, let's look at our introductory five basic positions.

I can't stress enough the importance of meditating between cast when using the 5 answer system. You are given information in the form of yes or no answers, for the most part but, there are always answers that lie in the 'empty' *between* space between your questions and their answers.

I've seen some internet posts that imply that 5 position OBI casting is inadequate. This is idiotic. This is a sacred system; all forms of it. When you enter the realm of the diviner and call on the support of all of the diviners and spirit workers who presently walk the planet and of ancient shamanistic energy, you're increasing your psychic prowess.

So, if you hear this idea that any form of Afrakan divination is useless, tell the false pretender to KICK ROCKS!

This is an exact science but, your work is not done once you finish this book and memorize the positions and their meanings; the more you heighten your awareness, the more you'll ovastand what the OBI are relaying to you. You'll find that in time some questions won't even need to be asked as the OBI positions will be in your head before the cast hits the surface.

Grasping the Root of Divine Power 97

In 5 position casting we are focusing strictly on light and dark segments. These are also referred to as open or closed segments.

The symbol for an open/light/"face-up" segment is "O".
The symbol for a closed/dark/"face-down" segment is "X".

We use this 5 position system to mainly ask yes or no questions but, through contemplation of the answers it also serves as a potent tool to sharpen our psychic sensibilities.

For these cast I suggest a fresh coconut to **start off** with. I actually advocate the storing of your casting materials so; allowing the coconut pieces to dry out and continuing to use them is permissible. They maintain your Ase and can be used for Adimu. Keep them in a consecrated place such as your Aforemuka.

*It should be noted that coconut are used as a kola nut substitute but, technically, and traditionally, are not "OBI". The actual Yoruba word for coconut is **"agbon"**. I suggest the use of coconut for the beginner diviner but, one's aim should be to utilize the original Kola nut oracle, if obtainable.*

5 THE HARD WAY

Akinmoran!
Akinmoran!
Akinmoran!

Alaafia - OOOO

The answer is "Yes".

This cast gives us an affirmative answer totally bathed in light. I liken this cast to a runner jetting out of the starter block...all systems are "go". There's clearly strength, vigor, ability, and sanctioning before takeoff.

Alaafia is a sign that signifies happiness, health, and general well being but, it should be innerstood by the reader that all things in life are duplicitous.

As Alaafia can represent the light and illumination of a blessing it can also come as a blinding light that causes us to lunge forward without proper grounding... or correctly taking root.

Accept the "Yes" that this cast indicates but, I strongly advise you to meditate on the answer and ask further questions as to the nature of the results because this "Yes" says good things could sour easily if the situation is not thoroughly measured and weighed.

5 THE HARD WAY

Etawa - OOOX

The answer is "Yes" or "No" depending on mutable factors.

The Etawa cast, in my opinion, gives the best opportunity for a beginner diviner to sharpen their skills of intuition.

Etawa speaks of there being a majority of active light force but, there exist one "unseen" variable that is affecting the manifestation of what could be.

This undetected variable could ,more than likely, be the person being divined for or a variable that seems insignificant but, is causing a blockage.

If your cast falls on Etawa you are then required to cast again.
If we receive Etawa we must cast again.
If you receive Alaafia, Ejife, or Etawa on the second cast the answer is "Yes".
If receive Okanron or Oyeku on the second cast the answer is "No".

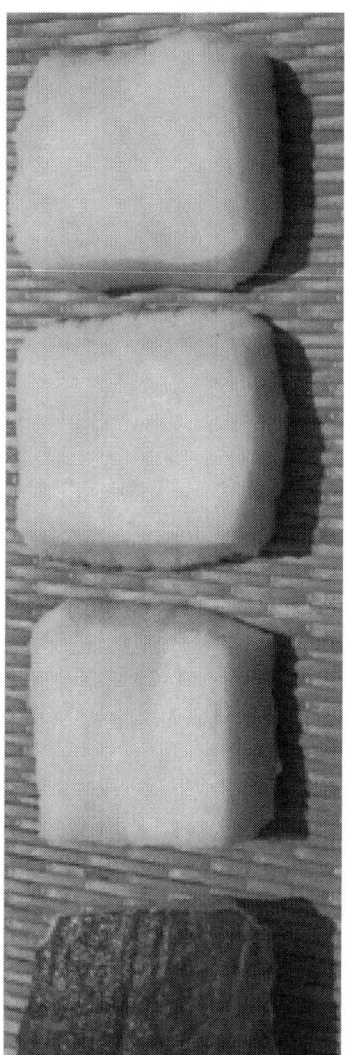

If you receive Etawa on your first cast and cast again pay very close attention to what you receive on the next cast.

The Etawa cast tells us that a concrete answer lays waiting for us but, first we need to give thought to some factors we may not be considering before that answer is revealed.

If, for example, you cast and receive Etawa and then cast again and receive Etawa; your answer would be "yes". Ask yourself why not Alaafia or Ejife on the second cast? Why Etawa again? This gives you a moment to meditate and connect with the energy you're casting to and raise your own perceptual vibration in order to ovastand the energies at play.

There are those who claim that Etawa is an answer that reveals uncertainty so, a cast must be made again; this is not a random science. The spirits are not uncertain about anything.

This cast position prompts the diviner (yes, that's you) to recognize that there are factors affecting the result of this query in either a negative or affirmative manner.
Etawa speaks of different possibilities:
The affirmative response
The negative response

Many times the contribution/effort of the person being cast for is *making the difference* in the cast result.

5 THE HARD WAY

Okanran XXXO

Answer is "NO".

Okanran is the inverse of Etawa. In this equation we see that darkness is predominantly present with one "seen" identifiable that is holding out ...or on its way out.

This cast lets us know that the light or active force is being overcome by dark or latent forces/situations.

The probability of success has become so narrow that one is advised to allow the situation to come to a close as a candle burning the last bit of its wick. It could be saved but, it may be best to turn in for the night and start fresh on a new path when the dawning sun appears to light new possible pathways to what you desire.

Ejife - XXOO

Answer is "YES".

Ejife is the most solid "yes" you can receive within the 5 cast system because it's a balanced answer; in that we have two segments of light and two segments of dark.

Ejife is like the Coltrane song "Equilibrium" where all things above are balanced with all things below. Imagine all things unseen being in harmony with all things seen. When this cast is received there's no need to pursue this line of questioning as your answer "yes" is concrete.

Do not ask further.

Oyeku - XXXX

The answer is "No".

The Oyeku cast is one that is often misunderstood as a cast that always signifies danger and should compel the diviner to end the season and consult an Orisa priest, Babalawo, or Iyanifa.

Before you go running into your nearest shrine... trippin', let's examine what this cast is saying to us.

As we see with this cast the situation being queried into is surrounded in complete darkness.

Let's think on the notion that sometimes *man's rejection can be the spirits* **protection**.

From a western racist perspective, things that are dark or black are evil. Innerstanding that good or evil are only subjective terms that morph and twist to the perception of the society assigning them, let's throw them out the window for a moment in order to open up our awareness.

Do not ask further.

Example Cast:

Should I sign up for the Kupigani Ngumi Martial Arts class in order to get in shape?

The first cast reveals **Etawa**
The second cast reveals **Ogbe**

This cast could possibly be expressing that signing up for the Kupigani Ngumi class will present an opportunity to get in shape but, perhaps you've had other opportunity's to get healthy and without the right amount of effort on your part this may represent another failed attempt.

No answer is wrong, only more or less informative.

5 position Questions Exercise -

Perform this exercise for 30 days.
Ask ONLY the following questions:

Am I in alignment with my spiritual destiny?

Are my love ones fairing well today?

Do my Ancestors require an offering?

Do I need to do a spiritual cleanse of my home?

Do I need to do a spiritual cleanse bath?

Does my ORI require an offering?

Record your results in the following format:

Date:
Question:
Result:

For example:

Date: 8/15/2010 (Roman time)
Question: Do my ancestors require an offering?
Result: OOXX

The Casting Surface

THE CASTING SURFACE

The Casting Surface-

Our casting surface should be clean and dedicated to the sole purpose of divination. I'd suggest a wood mat or a white cloth.

As with any divination work, ***do not hold the gift higher than the giver of the gift.*** In other words, the paraphernalia are wonderful tools to use that have been given to us from the spirits but, the focus should be connecting with the spirits not, possessing the most expensive mat or cloth to cast on or thinking we can't cast because we don't have a dedicated room in our home. When you chant and pour Tambiko, you make the casting area sacred.

For the purposes of our casting we'll be looking at the "Opon Ifa" used in Ifa divination.

The Opon Ifa is a representation of the universe as well as the "inner-verse". You do not need an Opon to cast OBI. You just need to visualize the flow of energy and recreate a universal representation wherever you cast. When I cast, I always make sure I'm facing north so as to interpret direction easily. You can even draw a casting surface on a wooden mat and create the same representation as you'll find on the diagram on the next page.

Grasping the Root of Divine Power

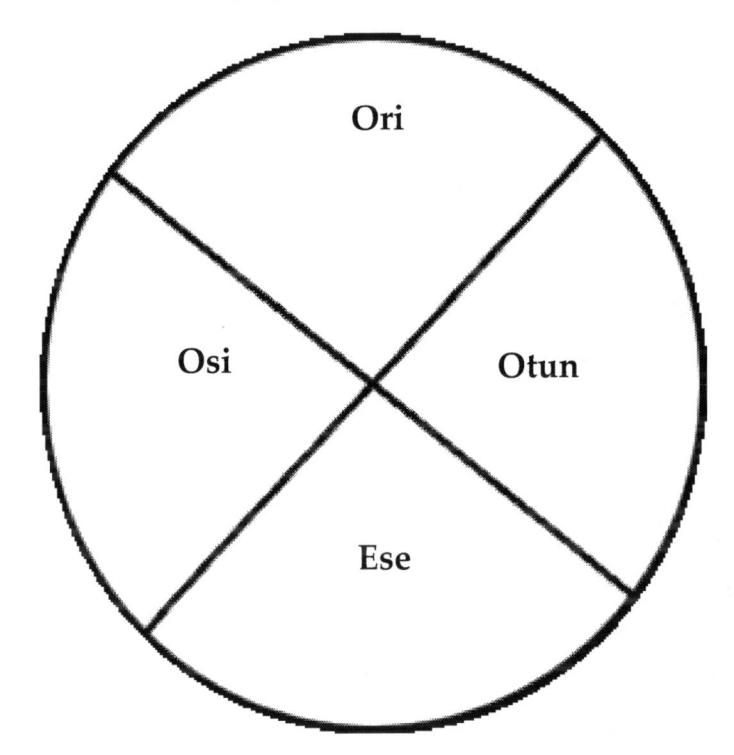

```
         Ori


  Osi        Otun


         Ese
```

Opon-Ifa

    This is our casting surface as outlined by the Opon Ifa. This is the divining tray of the Babalawo or Iyanifa and is used by the Ifa priest to prepare medicine.

    For our purposes we'll use this layout to not only cast our OBI but, to also innerstand how energy flows throughout our lives.

THE CASTING SURFACE

1) Ori-Opon

Energy -Metaphysical/Potential
This is the Northern or upper region of the casting surface/Opon-Ifa. This area represents the invisible realm better described as Orun. From this region we are granted the seeds of manifestations from our Egun and the Irunmole (those who dwell in "heaven"/Orun).

Element - Air
All things begin in this realm whether they conjured through thought or spiritual blessings/protection/seeds. This is the genesis of all things that we see with our physical eye. In this realm we enact the powers of our super-conscious and connect with our spirit body and spirit guides.

2) Ese-Opon

Energy - Physical/Kinetic Energy
This is the Southern or lower region of the casting surface/Opon-Ifa.

Element - Earth
This is where the seeds of potentiality fall from the "Ori" region, or Orun, and plant themselves.
This is the earth's crust, our place of toil and invested effort in the physical realm. This can be represented by our day to day activities (school, work, kwk...). This is where **"we use what we got to get what we want"**.

3) **Otun-Opon**

Energy - Materialization of Potential and Kinetic Energy
This is the Eastern region of the casting surface/Opon-Ifa.
Element - Fire
This is the realm that reveals the product of the cultivation and nurturing we gave to the seeds in the Ese region.
In the Otun quadrant we see the light of the new day. This is the place of the sunrise and our incarnation of success or failure. In this quadrant we move forward with surety and drive with the knowledge that we can eat of the rewards, good or bad, of the work that we've invested in the Ese quadrant.

4) **Osi-Opon**

Energy - Transformation of energy from three other quadrants
This is the Western region of the casting surface/Opon-Ifa.
Element - Water
This is the place of full transformation, physical death, and where the power of emotion is strongest.
In the Osi Quadrant we are made aware of the importance of change and the willingness to shed emotions, concepts, and ideas that no longer work in our best interest. This is a realm that reminds us that letting go of the past and embracing a more refined world view is needed in order to continue to elevate our perception.

THE CASTING SURFACE

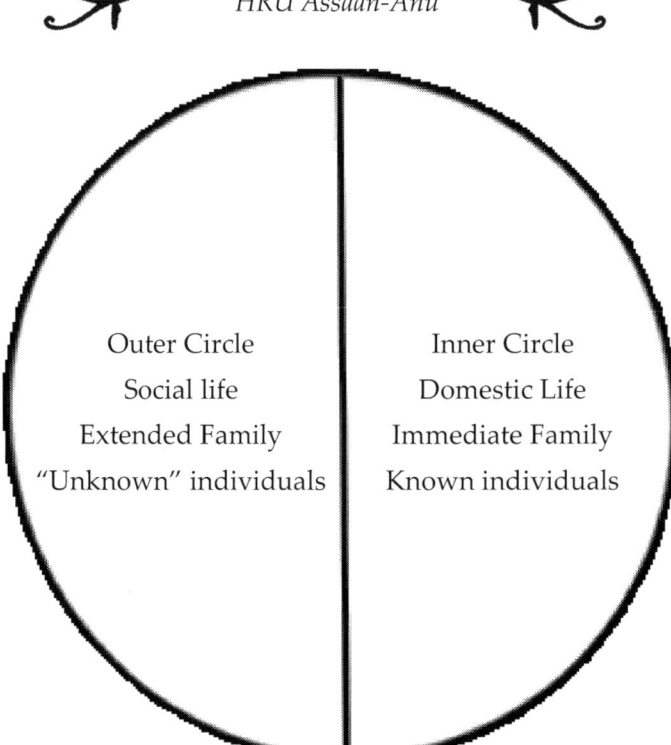

```
            Outer Circle    |    Inner Circle
            Social life     |    Domestic Life
         Extended Family    |    Immediate Family
        "Unknown" individuals |  Known individuals
```

Another consideration with our casting surface is the representation of the domestic life of the person being divined for and their social life.

The right side or eastern hemisphere of the casting surface represents the inner circle of the person being cast for. This would included home life, intimate relationships, immediate family, closest comrades, kwk...

The left side or the western hemisphere host the external social life of the client bring represented. This would include their work life, school, extended family members, communal affiliations; and unknown individuals who may have the ability to affect them in some way, kwk...

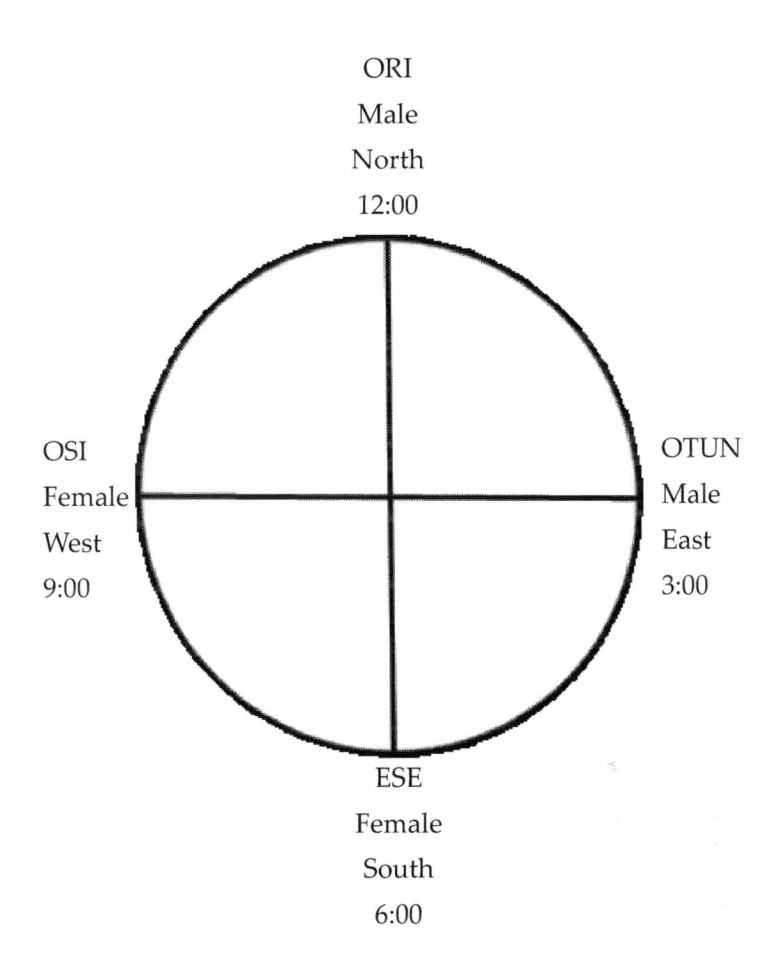

```
         ORI
         Male
        North
        12:00

OSI                      OTUN
Female                   Male
West                     East
9:00                     3:00

         ESE
        Female
        South
         6:00
```

Look at your casting surface and the movement of energy through the life of the individual in the formation of an upside down "4". We start in the north, then fall to the south, manifest in the East and shed in the west.

    Trace the movement with your finger.

THE CASTING SURFACE

Now let's talk about segments at home and segments in conflict.

Male Segments

A male segment is at home when it either falls or is pointing between 12:00 and 3:00. If it points directly to one of those cardinal points (12:00 or 3:00) it is considered to be representing the energy of that quadrant to the fullest.

Female Segments

A female segment is most at home when it falls or is pointing between 3:00 and 6:00. As with the male segments, if it points to its cardinal points (3:00 or 6:00) it is considered to represent the energy of its quadrant at maximum.

A segment at home is a good sign or as some say, "the Ifa is good". A segment pointing away from its home position is considered a frustrated or conflicted segment and points to a prospective or current challenge.

A segment that lands in one of it's at home quadrants but is pointing outside of its home zone is considered to be pulling the energy of that other quadrant into its own. Equally, I say this could also indicate that the energy that the segment symbolizes and what that particular home position represents may be leaving that quadrant as indicated by the segment orientation.

So now how does this explain the movement of energy?
I gatchoo, I gatchoo....
Here's an example:
1- **(ORI)** Nzinga and Kwame lay at their Jingili and send out request to establish a self sufficient eco-village in a rural area. This request is received by Esu, the divine messenger, and he creates an opportunity via the Ase of their prayers and Ancestral Ase pool. Esu presents them with the opportunity to go on a 12 month nationwide lecture tour teaching alternative power, sustainable building, and organic farming. By doing this they have the opportunity to raise the needed funds to buy the land and supplies needed for the eco-village.

2- **(ESE)** Kwame and Nzingah do the tour and travel throughout the country teaching the techniques and methods needed for sustainable living. They also distribute sign-up sheets for their mailing list for those who may be interested in investing in the eco-village.

3- **(OTUN)** At the end of the 12 month tour not only have they earned the needed funds but, they've also gathered a community of support and individuals who are invested in the idea of the eco-village and who desire to live there. These are people who can now demonstrate the skills that they've been taught and have done so in various workshops that the Afrakan couple are now hosting locally.

4 - **(OSI)** Now it is time to make the exodus from the sh*ty...I mean the city. This will entail leaving their jobs as financial

concubines….I mean "9 to 5'ers", trading in the luxury car for a 4x4 vehicle, taking the children out of the warehousing public fool institutions…I mean public schools and developing a home schooling curriculum, giving up certain western *creature* comforts and conveniences, kwk….

If they complete this 4 step process, all that they envisioned is theirs to grasp and claim ownership to because they've followed the proper process and it's manifestation was ordained in Orun. Can you dig it?

THE CASTING SURFACE

And the whole 9!

AND THE WHOLE 9!

And the whole 9! -

9 Position casting

In order to cast 9 position OBI segments in a way that is effective and informative the diviner must, first, have a thorough innerstanding of how the expressions of male or female segments reveal their own message. Whereas with 5 position casting the emphasis was on open/light or closed/dark segments; with 9 position we note our segments as open or closed, male or female, as well as the respective positions that each segment falls on our casting surface.

It's a significant realization that all things in this world have dual nature....light is not always a "good" thing and dark is not always a "bad" thing and vice versa. All energy conjoin for the purposes of advancing and upholding the order of life. There is no good , there is no bad; it is what it is. Focus on the science of "is-ness".

It's of the utmost importance that we now draw up what we've learned about male/female and light/dark interoperability in order to properly read our 9 position casts.

Segments that are considered light segments, those that are showing the actual gender of the OBI/white part of the coconut, are considered to be talking. These are called open segments.

The segments that show the dark side of the coconut, the back side of the OBI, are considered closed and referred to as "Ooya".

A closed segment can represent blockage or protection.
An open segment represents an active force.

It is customarily taught that the gender of an Ooya is disregarded and only the gender of the open segments is read. I do not follow this model as I feel that every nuance of the cast should be scrutinized so, I consider the orientation and gender of every segment on the casting surface. Let YOUR ORI guide.

It's important to note:

If an Ooya lands above a frustrated segment it brings a hindrance of some sort. If it falls under a frustrated segment it brings protection.

If an Ooya falls above a segment that is at home it brings protection. If an Ooya falls below a segment that is at home it represents a hindrance of that beneficial energy.

This is not a hard set rule and may change depending on the segment orientation and the energy of the cast. Use your intuition.

AND THE WHOLE 9!

Remember to always record your cast.

Record the following informaton:

Date
Question Asked
Open or Closed Segment
Direction that segments point to on the casting surface
Area of the casting surface that segments land

Aje

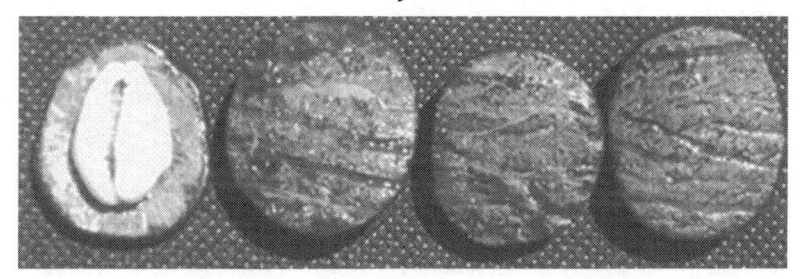

In harmony with the natural order:

Aje is a cast that foretells of the influx of wealth, peace, abundance, prosperity, and coolness into the life of the person being divined for.
One must focus their energy into the female/creative/watery aspects of their nature in order to fully exploit their feminine, emotive, or intuitive gifts. There is a warning here that one must use the power of intuition and sensation to deal with any new or preexisting situations/concerns. It is time to tap into the inner mystic and develop/utilize creative and psychic gifts.

In opposition to the natural order:

When not in alignment with the orientation of this energy your emotions will create a fog around you that will prevent you from "take off". You're so wrapped up in the psychic and emotive possibilities, or misinterpreted "signs", that you're not grounding yourself in solid pragmatic reasoning. Also one could be confusing emotional insecurities for intuition. One needs to dissolve feelings of self-importance and project their consciousness into a place above ego and insecurity.

AND THE WHOLE 9!

Ilera

In harmony with the natural order:

Ilera is a cast that foretells of the surety of victory, success, and notoriety in the life of the person being divined for. This is a time to drive forward with confidence and resolve. You may find yourself having to cut through the obstacles in your life in a way that pulls every strand of courage from you. Pay careful attention to where this open segment falls on your casting surface to see where to focus your ambition.

In opposition to the natural order:

When not in alignment with the orientation of this energy you'll find that too much unchecked male aggression is leading you into a place of misfortune and possibly even physical or mental peril. You're being too narrow-minded and failing to see the broader picture at hand.
This is a time to utilize the cooling energy of your feminine side.

Ejire

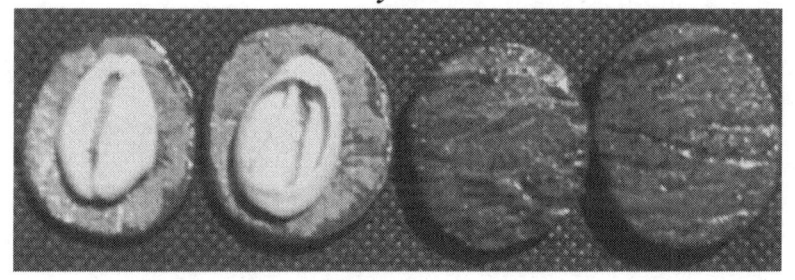

In harmony with the natural order:

Ejire's Ako and Abo segments remind the client that cooperation between the mind and spirit are key for one to actualize success and HARMONY.
The collaboration between masculine and feminine energies facilitates all creativity on the planet and beyond. The power to construct reality is present. Also Ejire could literally be pointing to positive results occurring because of a male/female joint venture.

In opposition to the natural order:

The intuitive/psychic/feminine energy/left brain is not in step with the rational/calculating/masculine energy/right brain in the inner/outer-spheres of the individual. The art of give and take is being under utilized. There is a myopic one-sidedness in the way the individual perceives the situation at hand. Male/female energy must regain their throne, be loosed in their manhood or wombmynhood respectively and be on one accord. Until this happens there will be no materialization of one's desires and no fruit yielded from effort invested.

AND THE WHOLE 9!

Ero

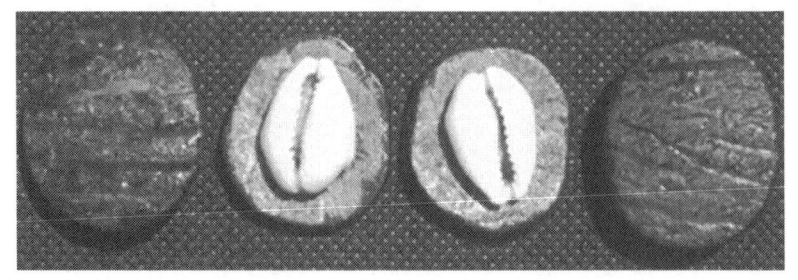

In harmony with the natural order:

Ero is a cast that foretells of peace, wealth, and plenitude entering the immediate circle of the person being divined for.
This cast relays coolness is on the way and the cooperation of psychic forces is at hand. Ero also signifies the need for psychic meditation and emotional stabilization. The internal waters of emotion are tranquil and this is a good time to study the reflections cast on their surface to learn about your emotional body. This sign signifies a quiet love affair with oneself and surroundings.

In opposition to the natural order:

This reveals one who may have become lazy and their feelings of entitlement are hindering their forward movements. The person being cast for is stuck in dreamland and is developing atrophy of movement. This cast in a conflicted state also speaks of one who is obsessing on one issue and that fixation is causing them to lose sight of what is important for the progression towards healing and enlightenment.

Akoran

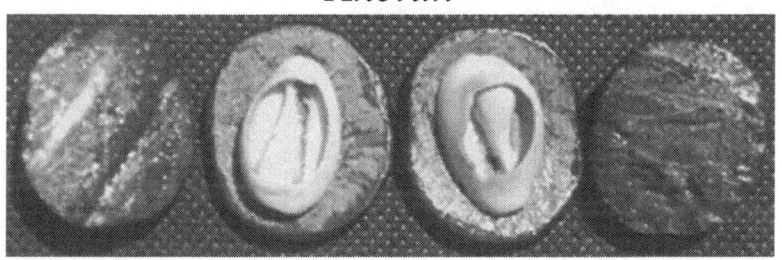

In harmony with the natural order:

Akoran foretells of success and victory in battle. This cast lets us know that either through struggle or cooperation with two male energies we will bring victory and advancement into our life experience.

One will soon chase away defeat through the use of courage and a tangibly high output of force. There may be two male energies present that assist in bringing out the highest level of performance in one another.

Moving forward with a cool head is recommended at this time.

In opposition to the natural order:

Confrontation and felonious behavior is nearby. A false sense of self has caused one to think they are invincible and can operate above the consequence of u-n-i-versal law.

Fear may also be an operative force. Not facing the true issue at hand and running has caused inferior forces to pursue with greater, unwarranted, confidence. Summon your outer/inner strength, breath deep, and face this illusion of danger. You are a child of the universe; nature is your bodyguard so, MAN UP.

AND THE WHOLE 9!

Obita

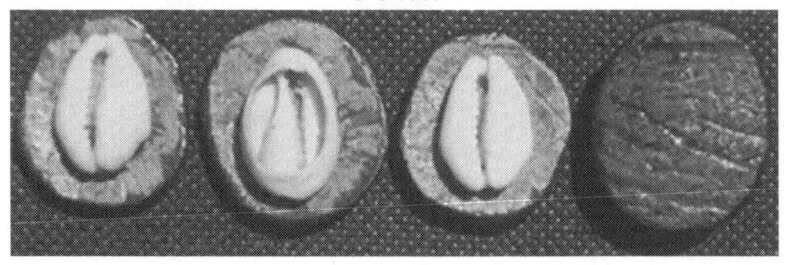

In harmony with the natural order:

Obita speaks of peace, harmony, and material gain being at hand. The inner circle, particularly home situation, is tranquil and flowing in a righteous direction. This solace is maintained by upheld virtue and the application of the science of sharing. This is a time that one feels the nurturing and receptive energy of the cosmos respond positively to their ability to align with healthy principles and people.

In opposition to the natural order:

Peace, tranquility, and happiness are scarce because adherences to virtue and proper morals have been abandoned. This may be a result of one being selfish and possessive or not doing their "share" to contribute to the upkeep of their home and domestic harmony. Character may also be in question. Possibly, this could signify two female energies failing to work in coalition in order to support a shared male interest. There may be an unhealthy level of competition stemming from feelings of insecurity and unwarranted ownership.

Akita

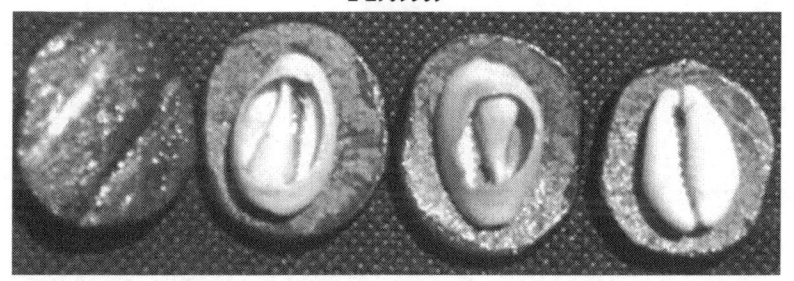

In harmony with the natural order:

This cast reveals a situation where suffering and misfortune are at hand but victory is achieved through perseverance of character and fortification of one's own inner truth. To maintain a harmonic balance with the universal forces that bring success, it is vital that one not allow the situation at hand to take them further out of their zone of sanity. It is time to stand firm on solid principles; such as the "14 Afrakan principles".

In opposition to the natural order:

The original aim of the war has been forgotten and the idea of the "fight" has becoming the motivating passion. Success and victory are blocked because of a combative "rebel without a clue" or misguided warrior.

This could also point to a situation where two hostile or male energies are contending over money, what is being perceived as an entitled reward, or a female energy. This unwholesome objectification is causing one to sink further into misfortune. The female segment reminds us wombmyn are wise enough to know when to humble and bow out. Follow her lead.

AND THE WHOLE 9!

Oyeku

In harmony with the natural order:

Oyeku (The "science of death") speaks of the process of shedding away layers or concepts that have outlived their purpose. It speaks of a transforming "death". Death is a necessary passage through undifferentiated matter (see the section entitled **"Too black, too Strong"**). Protection is being offered by an unseen force and one should meditate as to where that protection is coming from and give proper tribute. This is a cast that has a very strong Ancestral inference.

In opposition to the natural order:

There is a blockage and perhaps even danger and one should determine if that blockage is a form of protection, a self-generated hindrance, external blockage, or a "3rd party" covertly attempting to influence the person's life that is being divined for in a harmful way.

Do not continue in your line of question on this subject. Dip you OBI in cool water, saying "OBI tutu". When the cast is received there exist the likelihood of physical, mental, and/or spiritual injury. Seek the guidance of an Elder Awo (Priest/Priestess).

Ogbe

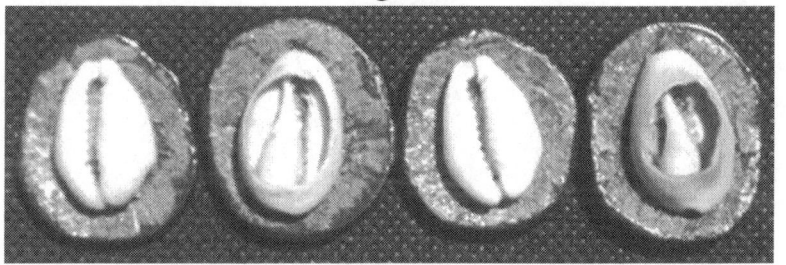

In harmony with the natural order:

Ogbe is a cast that yields a "yes" answer for what you are inquiring and reveals a straight and open pathway. This can be likened to a well trained Zulu Army preparing to launch a new battle campaign. The warriors are prepped and ready and the roadways are ready to receive them. This cast reveals a great creative energy and the possibility of travel soon. Ogbe expresses leadership, enlightenment, good health, and spiritual endowment.

In opposition to the natural order:

There are too many choices at hand and they are causing the person being divined for to be blinded by the options. This can be currently expressing itself in hyperactivity or even a pompous loftiness. With Ogbe, it is important to look at the surrounding circumstances of the situation. The person's character may be their downfall as this cast is one that focuses heavy on character cultivation. If things are not going well it is because one has not embarked on the journey and is spending too much time marveling over the choices.

AND THE WHOLE 9!

Sample 9 position cast:

Ogbe is a cast that yields a yes answer for whatever you are inquiring about but, is not necessarily a yes without strings attached. Ogbe proves an affirmative response but warns it is important to look at the surrounding circumstances of the situation.

For example:

The consultant ask if it would be possible to move into a larger apartment in the coming season and receives Ogbe as an answer.

It's important to look at the OBI's orientation to fully see what one should expect in making such a move.

The answer could be yes; in that you could move into a larger apartment but, does that really let us know if that move would be *most* advisable. You could move into the apartment and then discover that you're unable to afford the new/greater expense.

A more intelligent question may be posed this way:

"Would it be well advised for me to move into a larger apartment in the coming season" or "What would be the energy governing my decision to move into a larger apartment next season"?

Now that we are casting in a manner acknowledging the OBI positioning we can derive more from the OBI cast using the visual clues that we are provided with.

9 position casting exercise-

Perform this exercise for **30** days.
Ask the following questions **ONLY**:

What is the energy governing my day today?
What is the energy governing my spiritual walk today?

Record the following information for each cast:

Date
Question Asked
Segment Cast Result
Segment Orientation
Pictorial of cast using diagram like the one below

For Example:
8/17/2010 (Roman Time)
Am I in alignment with my spiritual destiny?
"Ejire"
OM- Pointing East in Ori quadrant
OF-Pointing South in OSI quadrant
XM- Pointing South in Ese Quadrant
XF- Pointing North in Ese Quadrant

AND THE WHOLE 9!

Orisa
"ORI"- Head
"Sa" - Selected

ORISA

Orisa

Orisa is a selected conscious within the realm of the supreme intelligence.

All things in the U-N-I-verse are aware and animate; even those objects that are inorganic. Everything has consciousness.

There are universal energies that govern the laws and character of the cosmos. These are called Orisa. Orisa are divine energies represented through nature's forces.

As mentioned previously, I strongly recommend the novice diviner focus their study primarily on the concept of Ori and Egun. What I will provide is a brief description of the Orisa known as **"The 7 Afrakan Powers"**. These particular Orisa are commonly found in many different Orisa/Nature based traditional Afrakan spiritual systems; as well as those of the Diaspora.

We, as humans, are in constant contact and negotiation with the Orisa; whether we realize it or not.

There are spirits of the Ocean (Yemoja), the Forest (Ogun), opportunity (Esu), Love (Osun), Leadership (Sango), Death (Oya), and Wisdom (Obatala) that we utilize and interact with daily. All of these Orisa/Energies work in coalition for the purpose of the whole unified consciousness.

Many claim that certain Orisa "*don't like*" other Orisa or some are engaged in eternal battle. In my humble opinion, I feel that some have misapplied the gift of anthropomorphic characteristic that were assigned to different Orisa so that our finite minds could grasp them, conceptually. The Orisa teach us how different energies manifest themselves at their fastest vibration (highest potential) and at their slowest vibration (deficient character).

The declaration that Orisa don't get along with one another is

Grasping the Root of Divine Power

an assignment of *human* discord and *human* unchecked ego.

When certain Orisa come into contact with one another the exchange can be explosive, just as when certain earth energies come in contact with one another there can be elemental transformations that can produce explosive results.

The Orisa, as all things in nature, work in coalition.

For example:

We aspire to Obatala for wisdom.

Esu opens the door to our transformation.

Osoosi points the way.

Ogun then helps us to overcome internal/external obstacles that might stand in the way of our transformation.

Sango gives us the courage to move forward and stay focused on the broader picture.

To provide further example:

There are many tales that describe the love triangle between Oya, Ogun, and Sango. Many state that because Oya was once married to Ogun but, was swept away by Sango the two brothers are engaged in eternal war. There is another way to see this.

Again, we must innerstand that there is an underlying symbiotic relationship that all Orisa share that must be innerstood and RAspected......

To illuminate this truth I'll use this tale as a reference but, superimpose the words of Carter G. Woodson, "**When you control a man's thinking you do not have to worry about his actions. You do not have to tell him not to stand here or go yonder. He will find his "proper place" and will stay in it.**" - This is an old mentality that is ingrained and deep rooted. In order to realize self actualization that "negro" needs to activate the OYA awareness

ORISA

in order to shed this mentality.

"**You do not need to send him to the back door. He will go without being told. In fact, if there is no back door,...**" - Ogun removed the obstacle of the back door/obstruction produced from a system of *supposed* white supremacy.

"**(con'td) he will cut one for his special benefit.**" - Because he doesn't know to pray to Sango to see the broader picture and for courage to move forward as result of being stripped of root culture.

Here Oya tells us the dying off of old programming is needed. This is where Oya activates as she holds the key to destroying and reprocessing what's no longer fruitful in our lives.

There was once the hindrance of a system that would not allow a person referred to as a "negro" to seek passage through the front door. WE know this front door represents right of entry to the fullness of humanity. So Ogun removes that obstacles and destroys the organism of "Jim Crow".

Now, courage is the requisite for the "negro" to stride through the door of transformation and retrieve their humanity. This is Sango's domain.

So Oya needed Ogun at one time to remove the obstacle but, then needs Sango to provide the courage for the recipient of this fortune to move forward to receive it.

There are other Orisa here at work but, this is a small example.

*In truth, The idea that sparked the notion that there was something beyond the programming that controlled ones actions came from Obatala as he is the creative /intellectual spark. The idea that one was even worthy of something better than what had been systematically design for them *came from the Orisa Osun. Esu provides safe passage along the way and also serves as the cohesive agent between the desire of the negro and the collective intention of the Orisa so; there is full cooperation between flesh and spirit.*

This is a very basic example of Ujiima amongst the Orisa.

Orunmila

Orunmila is the Orisa who brought Ifa, the laws of Oludumare, into this world. Orunmila is known as "**Eleri ipin Ibikeji Oludumare** - Witness to all choice of destiny second only to The Supreme Being". Although not the oldest of the Orisa, Orunmila was there when we decided our destinies and will know when we leave Aye, if we've realized those destinies or not. In nature Orunmila is represented by Palm nuts. Witness to Creation, Father of the Secrets, second only to Olodumare; Orunmila has an order of priest/priestesses called Babalawos/Iyanifas. They're devoted to divination and helping their community/clients avert death and harm through their ability to tap into visions of past, present, and future. Babalawos/Iyanifas are able to convey the intentions of Olodumare through the use of Ifa oracles (Opele, Ikin, and Opon Ifa) by consulting Orunmila.

I will not go into depth as to the character of Orunmila as the order of Orunmila is held by Babalawo's and Iyanifa. This segment is merely to make the reader aware of this powerful Orisa.

Attributes - Knowledge, Understanding, Wisdom, Spiritual devotion, Illumination, Prediction, Divination, Destiny, Character

Similar Energies - Thoth, Tehuti

Offerings - Clean fresh water, Gin, Kola nuts, Red Snapper, Plums, Corojo butter, White Wine, and Palm oil

Astrology - The fifth house Leo ruled by the sun

Number/s - 3, 21

Colors - Yellow and Green

Ewe - Guava, Sage, Night shade, Ginger, Dog bane, Guanine, Myrtle, Corn, Honeysuckle, Night Jasmine, Pitch Apple

Totem - Rat, Snail

Chakra - Brow

Reincarnations - Araba Aworeni Adisa Makoranwale

ORISA

Again, the information being presented here regarding the Orisa is basic and volumes upon volumes could be written about even one out of the hundreds...even thousands, of Orisa.

The following Orisa chapter is to serve as a basic primer to working with the Orisa but, again focus on your own ORI and Egun.
Remember, the Orisa are here to assist us in our journey towards freedom or free dominion.

- Use the Oriki to invoke the energy of the Orisa they belong to.
- Use the Ewe in order to create incense, charms, baths, or even teas for that Orisa
- Use the gemstones and place them on the chakra points assigned to those Orisa in order to activate that Orisa's energy within you
- Use the offerings listed for each Orisa to honor them through Adimu

The 7 Afrakan Powers

7 AFRAKAN POWERS

HRU Assaan-Anu

The 7 Afrakan Powers

There are an infinite number of Orisa operating in the universe. There are major Orisa that we can break down into seven basic complexes; Esu, Obatala, Yemoja, Ogun, Oya, Sango, and Osun.

Obatala - The thought/creative spark

Esu - The vehicle for transformation/the road/your traveling emissary

Ogun - The removal of ego/Our will to progress onward

Sango - The courage needed and faith in the unseen certainty of success

Oya - The transformation through death and reincarnation

Osun - The self confidence and creative force of our personal desires

Yemoja - The return to the source/healing/entrance into this phantom world

Obatala

The word "Oba" is typically translated to mean King but is actually an elision of "O" meaning spirit and "Ba" meaning male energy or in metaphysical terms expansive energy. Ancient Afrakans recognized the relationship between sunlight (spirit) and matter as Obatala is illumination. Obatala is the consciousness of creativity (the epitome of Kuumba) and the wisest of the Orisa.

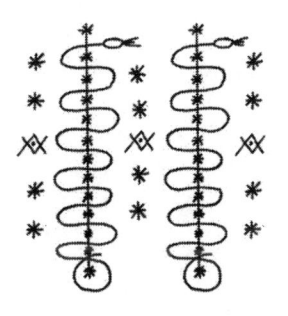

We commonly translate "Obatala" as "Oba" - Chief; "Tala" - White Cloth/Light

Obatala is the Chief of the white cloth/cloth. His white color (**not his skin**), containing all the colors of the rainbow, is created by adding equally proportionate colors of light in the color spectrum together. He is the white light which contains all colors and yet transcends them through his ability to objectively put all of their energies in proper perspective. He is the fabric/cloth that binds all things in Nature.

The Obatala consciousness is best perceived through learning and cultivating "Iwa Pele" and balancing Orisa consciousness in one's own body/mind temple. Obatala rules the mind, intellect, and creative energy. Obatala is the enlightened, keeper of that which is sacred; teaching us to respect our taboos and universal laws in order to align with our divine purpose. Obatala shapes the form of all humans on the planet.

Obatala reminds us of the dangers of overindulgence and a cloudy mind.

7 AFRAKAN POWERS

HRU Assaan-Anu

Attribute- Calmness, Contemplation, Meditation, Clarity, Creativity, Omnipresence, Illumination, Purity, Morality, Patience, Humility, "Eldership", Monogamy, Creativity, Higher Education/Awareness, Philosophy, Divine Law, Spirituality

Offerings - Coconut "Meat", White Pigeons, Cocoa Butter, Efun
Salt, Palm oil, and Palm wine should never be offered to Obatala

Body Components - Brain, Bones, White fluids of the body

Astrology - The ninth house of Sagittarius which is ruled by the planet Jupiter

Element - Earth (mountains)

Number/s - 8

Colors- White

Ewe - Feverfew, Garlic, Hyssop, Mint, Myrrh, Sage, Skullcap, Sage, Kola Nut, Basil, Blue Vervain, White Willow, Valerian

Totem - Snails, Elephants, Boa, Gorilla, Chameleon

Chakra- Brow (1st Eye), Throat

Gemstone- Calcite, Clear Quartz

Similar Energies - Ausar, Damballah, Tiembla Tierra, Brahma

Reincarnation - Imhotep, Haile Selassie, Dr. John Henrik Clarke, Mwalimu Bomani Baruti, Dr. Yosef Ben Jochannon

Oriki-

Oluwa Aiye or Oluwa Aye
Lord of the Earth
Alabalase
He who has divine authority
Baba Arugbo
Old Master or Father
Baba Araye
Master or Father of all human earth dwellers
Orisanla
The arch divinity

Esu -

Baba Esu is "Onibode" (the gatekeeper between

Heaven and earth); known by many names such as Tata Eleggua, Exu, Eshu, Elegba, Elegbara, Legba, and Papa Elegba.

Messenger of the Orisa, the guardian at the threshold between the physical and a metaphysical plain; Esu is everywhere. It is said Esu resides at the crossroad, opens and closes all doors, and shows multiple possibilities for our Path.

Esu serves as intercessory between those who dwell on the physical plain and the Orisa.

Esu is the steward of all Ase and owner of all the Ajogun (obstacles in life). Esu governs when sun, moon, or planet cross over into a various zodiac signs to assert a particular influence throughout the earth. This is an aspect of Esu working to ensure that the other Orisa are able to serve their purposes.

Esu is a good minister of Olodumare. He is the enforcer who ensures that due reward and punishment ensues on any action. He is, therefore, courted and even bribed. When such overtures fail to mitigate punishment, Esu is then given a bad name.

Esu is not the devil.

This is good ol' fashion christian missionary ignorance.

Call upon Esu in order to increase your wit, dexterity, and ability to see "both sides of a story".

Attribute - Segregation, Choices, Intellect, Creativity, Dexterity, Decisiveness, Objectivity, Follow-Through, Accountability, Cause and Effect, Communication

Offerings- Palm oil, Rum, Toasted corn, Dried fish, Jutia

Body components- Sympathetic nervous system, Para-Sympathetic nervous system

Astrology- The six house of Virgo ruled by Mercury; his influence may also be found in the third house as well.

Element- Earth (stones called "Yangi")

Number/s - 3

Colors- Red and Black

Ewe - Avocado, Chili Peppers (Jalapenos, Chiles, Habeneros, Serrano, Cayenne, Green Chilis, Poblanos, Cubans, KWK...), Cinnamon, Feverfew, Mint

Totem - Rat

Chakra- Root

Gemstone - Hematite, Black Tourmaline, Onyx

Similar Energies - Lucero, Set, Ganesh, Baphomet

7 AFRAKAN POWERS

Reincarnation - Araminta (Harriet Tubman), Richard Pryor, Johnny Cochran, Gil Scott Heron, Mutabaruka, Father Divine

Oriki -

Esu,
Divine Messenger,
Esu Odara,
Divine Messenger of Transformation,
Esu lanlu ogirioko.
Divine Messenger speak with power.
Okunrin ori ita,
Man of the crossroads
Ode ibi ija de mole.
Move beyond strife.
Ija ni otaru ba d'ele ife.
Strife is contrary to the spirit of Heaven.
To fi de omo won.
Unite the unsteady feet of weaning children.
Oro Esu to to to akoni.
The word of the Divine Messenger is always respected.
Ao fi ida re lale.
We shall use your sword to touch the Earth.
Pa ado asubi da.
Turn my suffering around.
No ado asure si wa.
Give me the blessing of the calabash.
Ase.
So be it.

Ogun

Ogun is the oldest warrior of blood and holder of Ire. Ogun is the blade that transforms the life of the being offered during ritual. Hence, it is recognized that Ogun always eats first at any moment of offering.

He is the head deity of Martial sciences and patron of civilization and technology. He governs technological progression, war, and forestry. Through his implements, Ogun teaches respect and humility by breaking down our egoic selves and helping us to realize the importance of charting new paths. Our own unchecked Ego is one of the obstructions to our fortune that we often, unknowingly, call upon Ogun to eliminate.

Ogun is able to remove obstacles out of our paths by his ability to break things down. He is the energy of analysis and scrutiny. Ogun uses his ability to get rid of obstacles that stand in the way of the flow of Ire into our lives; equally he removes obstructions in the flow of blood/light within our body temples. This signifies the symbiotic relationship that Ogun has with Osun. Osun is the energy that manages the flow of rivers and streams; much like the rivers of blood in our bodies and the stream of fortune that we desire in our lives. Ogun assist the work of Osun by removing any obstructions that may hinder her streams and rivers.

Ogun can assist in the curing of blood diseases.

Ogun's fiery red color represents the fullness of male virility and its expansive nature.

Ogun is also the owner of the forest domain. In the Yoruba

language the letter "O" signifies ownership. The word "Oogun" translates to "medicine". Medicine can be classified as matter that restores vitality or brings situations back into a state of equilibrium for right living. Ogun then can be innerstood as the determination to exist in balance; the will to carry on. This conviction is evident when we look at the industries that Ogun governs (forging, blacksmiths, martial science, agriculture, surgery). These are all areas of human involvement that are vital to the survival and continuance of civilization and culture.

Ogun is associated with the warrior planet Mars. In South Africa the biggest cultural group is the Kwa Zulu. The words Kwa Zulu are often translated into English as "we come from Mars".

Attribute - Ire, Force/Will, Martial Sciences, Technology, Patience, analysis, Metabolism (anabolic/catabolic), Movement, Impetus, Force, Patience, Hard work, Discipline, Dedication, Perseverance, Even-handedness, Level Headedness, Structure, Creativity, Mayhem, Destruction, Strength, Durability and Perseverance

Offerings - Palm Oil, Gin, Rum, Spears, Knives, Machete, Keys, Railroad Spikes, Roosters, Canines

Body components - Heart, Kidney (adrenal glands), Tendons, and Sinews

Astrology - The first house of Aries ruled by Mars

Element- Fire, Earth (forest), Iron, Steel (all metals)

Number/s - 3,4,7

Colors - Red, Green, Black

Ewe - Eucalyptus, Alfalfa, Hawthorn, Bloodroot, Parsley, Motherwort, Garlic, Mariwo (palm fronds), Peregun, Pine, Prickly Pear, Sunflowers , Chili Peppers (Jalapenos, Chiles, Habeneros, Serrano, Cayenne, Green Chilis, Poblanos, Cubans, KWK...)

Totem - Black Dog, Roosters, Goats

Chakra - Heart

7 AFRAKAN POWERS

Gemstone - Bloodstone, Hematite

Similar Energies - Hru-Khuti, Zarabanda, Ogou Ferraille

Reincarnation - Mike Tyson, Jack Johnson, Bumpy Johnson, Nat Turner, Colin Powell, Georgie Washinton Carver, Bobby Seales, The Deacons for Self Defense, Ben Carson, Frances Cress Welsing, François "Papa Doc" Duvalie, Imhotep, Hannibal

Oriki -

Ogun awo, Olumaki, alase a juba.
Spirit of the mystery of Iron, Chief of Strength, the owner of power, I salute you.
Ogun ni jo ti ma lana lati ode.
Spirit of Iron dances outside to open the road.
Ogun oni're, onile kangun-dangun ode Orun, egbe l'ehin,
Spirit of Iron, owner of good fortune, owner of many houses in Heaven, Help those who journey,
Pa san bo pon ao lana to.
Remove the obstructions from our path.
Imo kimo 'bora, egbe lehin a nle a benge ologbe.
Wisdom of the Warrior Spirit, guide us through our spiritual journey with strength.
Ase.
So be it.

Sango

(Xango, Sango, Chango) is a warrior, the Orisa of lightning, dance, drum, and enthusiasm. Sango is an amalgamation of the "red" aggression, and virility, of Ogun and the "white" equanimity of Obatala. He possesses the force of Ogun and the wisdom of Obatala. Because of his ability to contemplate and tap into his creative potential he can resolve any challenge with inventiveness while keeping cooler than the cool side of a pillow on a hot summer's night. Although Ogun is the most feared and fiercest warrior of the Orisa pantheon; Sango is the most *skilled* warrior. Strategy and skill is his realm.

He teaches us that action is necessary to bring about balance but that action must be enacted with a cool head and a well thought out plan. Sango ,also, teaches us to creatively find ways to overcome our enemies and challenges. Sango puts your faith to the test and holds you to your words. Like his brother Ogun, truth and evenhandedness are extremely important to him. Sango provides us with the courage to traverse the transforming experiences in life...embracing the needed *****deaths*** (*he is the husband of Oya).

Through the courage of Sango of we are able to accept the personal power that comes from developing our Ase, as is the primary goal of Orisa devotion. Some folks are scared of their own power....not Sango!

Sango is the lord of lightening and his lightening illuminates the darkness instantly. Sango is the light we experience at the moment of enlightenment. Sango's lightning bolt from on high

7 AFRAKAN POWERS

exposes, in an instant, all uncovered forces lurking amongst us.

The Sango awareness forewarns of the destructive/creative power of our words. He possesses a fiery temper and can produce words and statements that can cause irreparable damage.

Sango is the beauty and pleasure of manhood and represents the intensity of experience. He loves the ladies and makes no apologies about it as they also love his charm and virility.

If charm, courage, diplomacy, or rightful action is needed; Sango is the Orisa to honor and invoke.

Sango's symbol is the oshe, a double bladed axe.

Attribute - Introspection, Manliness, Vigor, Truth, Righteousness, Morality, Justice, Courage, Strategy, Versatility, Flexibility, Passion, Leadership, Upheaval, Rebellion, Uprisings of the enslaved/oppressed, and Sudden unexpected events.

Offerings- Red Apples, Red Palm Oil, Bitter Kola, Rooster, Ram

Body components- Reproductive system (male), Bone Marrow, Life force/Moyo

Astrology- The eleventh house is the house of Aquarius dominated by ruled by Uranus

Element - Fire, Lightning

Number/s - 6

Colors - Red, White

Ewe -Angelica, Chili peppers (Jalapenos, Chiles, Habeneros, Serrano, Cayenne, Green Chilis, Poblanos, Cubans, KWK...), Dandelion, Eucalyptus, Nettles, Cinnamon, Plantain, Saw Palmetto, Hibiscus, Fo-Ti, Sarsaparilla, Nettles, Cayenne

Totems - Horses, Black cat

Chakra- Solar plexus, Root

Gemstone- Carnelian

7 AFRAKAN POWERS

HRU Assaan-Anu

Similar Energies- Hru, Petro Lwa, Erzulie Dantor, 7 Rayos

Reincarnations - Shaka Zulu, Muhammad Ali, Dr. Khalid Muhammad, Nat Turner, The Black Panthers, Jean-Jacques Dessalines, The enslaved Afrakans in my only family who slaughtered their white slave-maker for violating my great-great-great grandmother (*as passed down from the wombmyn in my family*).

Oriki-

Alaafin, ekun bu, a sa
Alaafin, (the king of Oyo) snarls like a leopard and the people run away
Eleyinju ogunna
One whose eyeballs glow like charcoal
Olukoso lalu
Olukoso, the famous one of the city
A ri igba ota, segun
One who uses hundreds of cartridges to win victory in war
Eyi ti o fi alapa segun ota re
One who used pieces of broken walls to defeat his enemies
Kabiyesi o
We honor you
Ase
So be it

Oya

Oyá is the energy of storms, lightning, tornados, hurricanes and cemeteries. Also known as Yansa, Oyá is the master of transformation and the reassigning of power. She is the emissary and protector of the Egun. She transports the spirits of the recently deceased to the spirit realm. Oyá leads us to innerstand the science of death. She knows that all things must die in order to *transcend their form* and provides us with the fortitude to go through the doors of death in order to alter our structure.

Oyá is the wife of Sango and in that union she offers us the courage to accept the change in our lives. Reflective of the Sango/Oya union is the power relationship between a King who has the ability to enforce proper code and the insight to humble himself to the wise counsel of his equally powerful Queen. Oya serves as the one wombmyn confidant and advisor to Sango. She ruled the kingdom Oyo through her husband Sango. In nature, Oyá's guidance is still present as the *leader* electric discharge that scientist have discovered strikes the exact location at a fraction of a second before the greater electrical discharge, known as lightening, strikes (*Sango uses his lightening to clear and destroy what needs to be broken down*). Oyá still guides her beloved King.

Keep in mind that Oya is the energy of the wind and Sango is the energy of fire. Too much wind will cause fire to blaze uncontrollably. When Sango relied too much on the wisdom of Oyá he caused unrecoverable damage to his kingdom.

Oyá is a wombmyn of the market place and is keen to the

art of manipulation and advancement. Once married to Ogun she was able to learn the science and implements of warfare. Ogun even crafted, for her, the sword of correctness that she carries. After she left Ogun for Sango she was able to learn the discipline of the Obatala energy; as Sango has the raw power of Ogun and the wisdom of Obatala.

*Warrior Queen Hatsepshut was the 5th pharaoh 18th dynasty and was known to wear a beard and dress in male garb as she was respected as a fierce warrior and ruler. Oyá is also called "the one who puts on pants to go to war" and "the one who grows a beard to go to war".

Attribute - Transformation, Regeneration, Death, Sex, Reincarnation, Ancestors, Clairvoyance, Usurping of power; inheritances and the marketplace, Compassion, Sincerity, Dedication, Loyalty, Leadership, Level-headedness

Offerings - Purple Eggplants, Palm Oil, Rum, Gin, Red Wine, Hen, She-goats, Sheep, Locust, Black Horsehair, Switches, Copper, Plums, and Grapes.

Body components - Lungs, Bronchial passages, Mucous membranes

Astrology - The eighth house of Scorpio ruled by Pluto

Element - Fire, Air (wind/tornado/hurricane/whirl wind), Thunder

Number/s - 9

Color/s - Red, Maroon, Orange, Purple

Ewe - Mint, Passion flower, Rose, Rosemary, Texas Mountain Laurel, Yarrow, Bald Cypress, Bladderwrack, Damiana, Mullein, Comfrey, Cherrybark, Pleurisy root, Elecampane, Horehound, Chickweed

Totem - Buffalo

Chakra - Solar plexus, Root

7 AFRAKAN POWERS

HRU Assaan-Anu

Gemstone - Amethyst, Obsidian

Similar Energies- Nekbet, Manman Brigitte, Erzulie Dantor

Reincarnations - Assata Shakur, Yaa Asante Waa, Nzingah, Hapsetshut, Winnie Mandela, Queen Nandi, Adelaide L. Sanford

Oriki -

Ajalaiye, Ajalorun, fun mi ni ire,
The Winds of Earth and Heaven bring me good fortune,
Iba Yansan,
Praise to the Mother of Nine,
Ajalaiye, Ajalorun, fun mi ni alaafia,
The Winds of Earth and Heaven bring me well-being,
Iba Oya,
Praise to the Spirit of the Wind,
Ajalaiye, Ajalorun, winiwini,
The Winds of Earth and Heaven are wondrous,
Mbe mbe ma Yansan,
May there always be a Mother of Nine,
Ase.
So be it.

Yemoja

She is the primordial mother; sentinel of childbirth, children, wombmyn, and fertility. Yemoja is the original Wadjet and ruler of the ocean and moon. She rules the super-conscious mind; the internal dominion of creation within our own body temples. She is the mystical unknown enticing us to explore.

Yemoja's compassion is a healing force. She is the power of regeneration and healing.

Despite her propensity to nurture and care, she is a fierce and unforgiving warrior. Her salt waters are curative but, can also devastate the largest and greatest of vessels.

Yemoja's waters can be a womb in one moment and a tomb the next. This duality teaches that there is a time to be stern and a time to be strict; a time for compassion and a time for apathy.

Yemoja gives us the tending and support that is needed in order to recover from the pain and struggle of our life journey.

Yemoja provides us with the opportunity to gain wisdom/experience from the knowledge offered to us by Obatala by, guiding us through our transitions like an adoptive mother. Yemoja embodies the thought **"All children are OURS"**. To her, the "orphan" or "step-child" model is non-existent.

Yemoja is a gateway to Aye. She governs the amniotic waters that nurture and sustain life as one is fashioned and prepared for interdependent life on earth. Though Osun motivates conception it is Yemoja who ensures that every child receives the care and investment needed for development.

Attribute - Maternal, Domestic issues, Protective, Nurturing, Instinctive, Responsibility, Duty, Discipline, Healing, Regeneration, Jegna

Offerings - Watermelon, Mirror, Comb, Bermuda grass, Florida grass, Sponges, Coralline, Salt water rushes, Powders, Perfumes, Fruits, Molasses, Water Hyacinth, Seaweed, Purple Basil, Green Pepper, Chayote fruit, Cowry

Body components - Womb, Liver, Breasts, Buttocks

Astrology - The fourth house of Cancer ruled by the moon.

Element - Water

Number/s - 7

Color/s - Blue, White, Green

Ewe - Kelp, Squawvine, Cohosh, Dandelion, Yarrow, Aloe, Spirulina, Mints, Passion flower, Wild Yam root, Bladderwrack, Prickly pear, Rose

Totem - Fish

Chakra - 2nd (reproductive organs)

Gemstone - Azurite, Blue Lace Agate, Rose Quartz

Similar Energies - Auset, La Sirene, Mami Wata, Madre de Agua

Reincarnations - Marcus Mosiah Garvey, Kwame Nkrumah, Elijah Muhhamed, Queen Mother Audley E. Moore, Mother hale (Clara Hale), Black Panther Party for Self Defense (Breakfast program aspect)

Oriki -

Agbe ni igbe're ki Yemoja Ibikeji odo.
It is the bird that takes good fortune to the Spirit of the Mother of the Fishes, the female divinity of the Sea.
Aluko ni igbe're k'losa, ibikeji odo.
It is the bird Aluko that takes good fortune to the Spirit of the Lagoon, the Assistant to the female divinity of the Sea.
Ogbo odidere i igbe're k'oniwo.
It is the parrot who takes good fortune to the Chief of Iwo.
Omo at'Orun gbe 'gba aje ka'ri w'aiye.
It is children who bring good fortune from Heaven to Earth.
Olugbe-rere ko, Olugbe-rere ko, Olugbe-rere ko,
The Great One who gives good things, the Great One who gives good things, the Great One who gives good things.
Gbe rere ko ni olu-gbe-rere.
Give me Good Things from the Great One who gives Good things
Ase!
So be it.

Osun

Oluwa Awo Inu Didun Ipilese (the Owner of the Mysteries of the Pleasure Principle).

Yeah...sooo..sorry Miss Jackson but, Mama Osun put that down before you were hopping over chairs and doing the "Wop" in the old dance studio.

Osun is a beguiling lover of sweet things and of all that is beautiful. She is the owner of fresh water rivers and the rivers of blood which flow through our veins. She is a powerful enchantress and healer; just as the honey is that she loves so dear. This provides her with an exceptional gift of diplomacy. She's the only Orisa able to get the 24 hour eating and working Ogun to stop in his tracks and value her exquisiteness and magnetism. Osun is the law of attraction and governs the raw primal magnetism that occurs between forces and individuals.

Osun is not only wombmynhood and all of the alluring sensuality of it but, she is also the true mirror of manhood. She is the reflection of the highest love that man can express. She is the allure of procreation and man's desire to seek balance and achievement with his feminine complement. Osun is the reflection of pleasure and pain that man witnesses in the eyes of his mate.

Osun is the original gatherer of light and expresses her Ase through her capacity to form unions and nations. She instills racial and ethnic pride and promotes the ideas of nationalism and unity.

Osun favors the guinea hen; the same hen that Obatala used in order to scratch up the solid earth and spread it across the waters of the world. In this the Guinea hen created the platform for the nations of the world to form and develop. She is the great unifier.

Her symbol is the mirror, which is one weapon in her arsenal of many, because she knows how to astral travel with it.

She favors the pleasure of the senses and all forms of love.

HRU Assaan-Anu

Attribute - Love, Amalgamation, Nationalism, Umoja, Elegance, Beauty, Grace, Artistry, Charm, Charisma, Refinement, Materialism, Law of attraction/creation, Abundance, Motherhood, Wealth, Partnerships, Balance, and Harmony

Offerings - Honey, Brass, Gold, Copper, Pumpkins, Squash, Cinnamon, Oranges, Eggs, Cowrie shells, Perfume, Jewels, Peacock feathers, Bells, Five-pointed star, Fans, Fresh water, Anything artistic & beautiful.
Also five jars of honey, five oranges, five eggs, or five pumpkins

Body components - Circulatory system, Digestive organs, Elimination system, Pubic area (female)

Astrology -
The seventh house of Libra
The second house of Taurus

Element - Water

Number/s - 5

Colors - Gold, Green

Ewe - Sunflower, Calendula, Cinnamon, Damiana, Lavender, Rose, Yellow Dock, Burdock, Anis, Raspberry, Yarrow, Chamomile, Lotus, Uva-Ursi, Buchu, Myrrh, Echinacea

Totem - Peacock, Vulture, Cricket

Chakra - Navel

Gemstone - Carnelian, Coral, Agate, Brown Jasper (orange stones), Blue Calcite, Aquamarine, Copper

Similar Energies - Het-Hru, Mami Wata, Erzulie Freda

Reincarnations - India Arie, Kola Boof, Bob Marley, Erykah Badu, Barry White, Fela Kuti

Oriki -
Osun awuraolu.
The Spirit of the River, turtle Drummer.
Serge si elewe roju oniki.
Open the path of attraction, Mother of Salutations.
Latojoku awede we mo.
Cleansing Spirit that cleans me inside and out.
Eni ide ki su omi a san rere.
The maker of brass does not pollute the water.
Alode k'oju ewuji o san rere.
We are entitled to wear the crown that awakens all pleasure.
Alode k'oju ewuji o san rere.
We are entitled to wear the crown that awakens all pleasure.
Alode k'oju ewuji o san rere.
We are entitled to wear the crown that awakens all pleasure.
O male odale o san rere.
The Spirit of the Earth that wanders freely.
Ase!
So be it.

Methodology:

The way you work with the Orisa will be ultimately determined by your own character and style. We all approach divinity and the mundane in our own way.

For example:

When I work with Ogun, I find my cause is most aligned with Baba Ogun if I have hard-core hip-hop playing while I'm doing my rituals and incantations. Groups like Mobb Deep, M.O.P., Gangstarr, Public Enemy; and artist like Tupac, Biggie, Coremega, and Rakim provide the ideal spur for the vigor that I invoke through the Ogun awareness. This sound vibration helps me to preserve my "edge" and feeds my ferociousness reminding me that I'm a frontline RBG warrior....who will never retire his spear.

Playing Coltrane when working with Obatala works great for me.

For some this would seem blasphemous. I do what is effectual for me and follow the request of the spirits who work with me; I recommend you find your "groove" as well.

METHODOLOGY

HRU Assaan-Anu

So Fresh and So Clean Clean!

Included are some very basic ways to clean yourself, your environment, and stimulate your spirit body through the use of baths, incense, and mixtures for cleansing your home.

Incense

* Store all incense in glass containers.
* Powders should be burned on NON-TOXIC charcoal. Place the powder on the Charcoal once it burns to white.

7 Afrakan Power

- 4 table spoons of Frankincense
- 3 table spoons of Myrrh
- 2 table spoons of Cinnamon Powder
- 1 table spoon of Sage Powder
- 1 table spoon of Sandalwood Powder
- 1/2 table spoon of Dragon's Blood Powder

Use this incense and pray for balance throughout your entire being when you feel disjointed and out of tune with "01". This is good to burn while meditating or reciting your Oriki/Ofo Ase/Adura.

Home Tranquility

- 3 table spoons of Cinnamon
- 2 table spoons of Cedarwood
- 1 table spoons of Pine Resin
- 1 table spoons of Lilac Flowers

Use this incense to balance the energy in your home and bring tranquility. This is especially helpful if there has been a disturbance in your home or a foreign energy has recently visited/invaded your living space.

Dispelling directed harmful Energy

- 3 table spoons of Dragons Blood
- 1 table spoons of Rue
- 1 table spoons of Rosemary
- 3 drops Sage Oil

Burn this if you feel there has been some harmful energy directed towards you. Pray to your ORI, the Egun/Lidlotis/Nananom Nsamanfo, and the Orisa for protection and the ability to rise above what/whoever is attempting to harm you. DO NOT attempt to use this mixture to cast a harming spell on someone. **You'll shoot your eye out!**

Bath

Some of us live in an awfully unhygienic environment. There is spiritual sludge and biological grime that abound everywhere. The need for regular detoxing and cleansing is a direct result of a compromised environment. Here I will provide some basic baths for protection and cleansing.

Placing a cup of sea salt in your bath water is always an excellent way to cleanse yourself of foreign spiritual energy. Rose water, Lavender Water, and Florida Water are also choice cleansers and I would advise using either one of those every time you bath.

I would advise that whenever you enter your dwelling from outdoors you rinse yourself with a purification formula. It doesn't have to be a full bath but to mist yourself upon arrival with a spray bottle would benefit your spiritual well-being as well as those living with you, greatly.

SO FRESH AND SO CLEAN CLEAN!

Spiritual Cleanse/Quickner

- 3 fluid ounces of oil of Bergamot
- 1 fluid ounce of oil of Lemon
- 1 fluid ounce of oil of Ylang Ylang
- 1/2 fluid ounce of oil of Lavender
- 20 drops of oil of Cinnamon
- 12 drops of oil of Cloves
- 10 drops of oil of Neroli
- 1 gallon of Alcohol
- 1 pint of Rose Water

This can be used to wash sacred objects in your home or even sprinkled on charms in order to strengthen and quicken their intention. This is a very, very powerful bath so use it with sobriety.

Aura Strengthener/Spiritual Protection

- 1 Gallon of Spring Water
- 3 table spoons of Honey
- 4 cups of Orange juice
- 1 cup of Vinegar
- 6 table spoons of Sea Salt
- 6 drops of liquid extract Yarrow

This bath can be used to reverse the harmful effects of a hex or draining experience. This will rebalance your energy and strengthen your aura.

Floor/Home Wash

While using these washes one should focus on the objective for using them. If you're dispelling harmful energy then you should be focusing your mental attention on that aim or even chanting that purpose out loud.

Banishment

1 cup Sage
1 cup Rosemary
1 cup Lime Juice
1 cup Rue
1 cup Rock Salt
Rose Water

This is good when you need to clear your space of injurious energy and create an uninhabitable environment for adverse spiritual forces.

Protection

1 cup Pine Needles
1/2 cup Cloves
1/2 cup Cinnamon Sticks
1 cup Sage
1 tablespoon of Quartz Crystals
Violet Water

Use this wash if you suspect there is mischievous energy being directed towards your home. Open windows/doors when washing with this wash.

SO FRESH AND SO CLEAN CLEAN!

Purification/Consecration

1 cup of Sun Flower Petals
1 cup of Passion Flowers
1 cup White Carnations
1 cup Kosher Rock Salt
Rose Water

Use this wash to purify the space in which you house your Jingili/ Aforemuka.

7 Afrakan Powers

1 cup Abre Camino herb
1 cup Gardenia Flowers
1 cup Violets
1 cup Rosemary
1 cup Peppermint
Rose Water

Use this wash when you need to create money, love, and fortune in your life. This is also a good wash to engage and activate your own inner forces to manifest those desires in your life.

*Add 2 cups of any of these washes to 2 gallons of water and use them to wash the inside of your residence or business. You can douse the walkway leading up to your home or business with any remaining solution.

SO FRESH AND SO CLEAN CLEAN!

Conclusion

So there you have it.

You now have all of the tools needed in order for you to initiate your task of spiritual reclamation.

This is not a guide to microwave religion. As an Afrakan, *you* are religion. You need no special day to rise as the deity you are. You can choose now to begin the journey to return home. It will be a long process filled with emotional, psychic, and physical pains and struggle; and ,at times, it will be a very lonely walk. Despite the danger of this passage there is nothing more significant in this life journey than to ascertain the entirety of "you".

Divine power should never be chased as if it were some elusive obtainment to be hunted and caged. Divine Power should emanate from within and all of the techniques described in this work should serve to resuscitate the spiritual giant that lies within the consciousness of all Afrakan people. We are the original truth holders of the planet and we are the first to negotiate and establish agreement with natural/celestial entities. When approaching this information; approach with a purified mind. Your brain serves as a gateway to the cosmic world, when functioning as it should. The mind synthesizes experiences and information that some would call esoteric while storing the sacred routes in our cerebral databanks in order for us to return to the cosmic wormholes of higher awareness. On the other hand for those who have been scarred by the horrific onslaught of white supremacy; sadly, your mind is not your own. There is a "middle man" that reinterprets all of your life experience's for the purpose of shaping an ideology that will work in the best interest of your historical enemy. This, consequently, arrests your development in a place of perpetual confusion and internal turmoil and contention.

Those who came before, and still walk in front and behind you are calling from both sides of the water's shore. You are the u-n-i-verse's favorite child and your blood heredity provides you a medium and Black-print for course-plotting through this existence and the next. Regardless if you decide to take this Ancestral charge with seriousness, or not, there are many individuals/groups of alien races who are learning the sacred sciences of your racial and cultural origins and using them ritualistically and unceasingly, against you.

Your divine power is your beautiful Black self but, you must gain awareness of who/what that is. This is unfeasible within the context of an alien's outlandish fantasy religion. Don't be fooled by claims of the homogeny of all cultures/people (or what *appear* to be people) on the planet. This is a tool of manipulation intended to march you into a colorless, shapeless, rhythm-less, soul-less, anti-nature, powerless, decrepit state of mind. **Resist!**

It's time to be who your Ancestors fought for you to be, unapologetically. You don't have to provide just explanation to anyone for empowering yourself by use of Ancestral wisdom and divine guidance.

Walk in Beauty and Strength!

Your Brother in Victory,

HRU

*For those of you who are followers of IFA, you'll notice that the sacred ODU's are absent from this work. This was not an oversight but, done with prudent deliberation. The ODU are sacred portals to and from the ethereal. They give birth to fortune and misfortune and should not be invoked except for under the competent supervision of an Elder spirit worker.

In forthcoming works; I will cover ODU as well as more in depth rituals for the more advanced energy workers.

CONCLUSION

Glossary

Innerstand - I use this term as it relates to knowing and applying what is known. The aim is to have this knowing/experience of knowing exist internally. One does not want to be oppressed by being put "under" knowledge (understanding) but, one should be empowered at their inner core by it.

Ovastand - To "ova-stand" is to see the larger picture at work amongst the components that comprise that picture.

Ra - From the Kemetic pantheon the deity "Ra" represents divine light and the distribution of knowledge.

HRU - The son of Auset and Ausar in the kemetic Pantheon. HRU translates into english as "That which is above" or "Heavan". HRU's primary objective is to restore Ma'at.

Opon Ifa - Yoruba term referring to the diving tray used in the IFA system by Babalawo to mark ODU and make medicine.

Obi - Kola nut. The OBI are used for offerings and divination.

Adimu - Yoruba term referring to offerings given to Orisa and Egun.

Aforemuka- Twi term from West Afraka translated as "Altar/Shrine".

Jingili - Gulimancema term from West Afraka translated as "Altar/Shrine".

Tambiko - Ki-Bantu term describing the act of pouring libation.

Afrakan - One who possesses the divine light, spirit, and melanin content as reflected by the original people of the planet and who are conceptually and geographically associated with the Afrikan continent.

Afrakalogy - The study of the entire Afrikan continent for the purpose of assimilating the highest ideas of the Pan Afrakan experience.

Jegna - (Jenoch, plural form) Jegna is an Amharic word describing those special people who have (1) been tested in struggle or battle (2) demonstrated extraordinary and unusual fearlessness, (3) shown determination and courage in protecting her/her peoples, land and culture, (4) shown diligence and dedication to our people, (5) produced an exceptionally high quality of work, and (6) have dedicated themselves to the protection, defense, nurturance and development of our young by advancing our people, place, and culture.

-Wade W. Nobles ("From Na Ezaleli to the Jenoch")

Wombmyn - The Afrakan adult matured female.

Smudge - The use of smoke derived from plant/herbal substances in order to invoke an alternate state of awareness or to banish harmful energy from a space.

Innerverse - The internal reflection of all that exist external to one's own perception. There is nothing created or existent outside of one's own awareness that has not been birthed from that same internal consciousness. If you are aware of something it is because you have first fashioned it in your own "inner-verse".

U-N-I-verse - The space that lies in between all recognizable matter that connects all things in existence to one another.

Frankincense - Tree resin used for spiritual ritual. Ingested; the resin is also used for digestion and healthy skin (this is a clear grade of Frankincense that is chewed and is unlike the commonly sold frankincense).

Frankincense is used for treating arthritis, healing wounds, strengthening the female hormone system, purifying the atmosphere from undesirable germs, and repelling mosquitoes. Frankincense is also used to facilitate mediation and cleanse the home of harmful energy.

Kemites would ground the charred resin into a powder that was used to mark the eyes as black eyeliner.

It is a high vibration tree substance. Use liberally!

Myrrh - The word "Myrrh" derives from the Aramaic word "Murr" translated into english as "bitter".

It's made from dried tree resin and is used for spiritual cleanses, focus, and offerings.

Myrrh is also used as a rejuvenating tonic, mouthwash, tooth cleaner, and analgesic. It's also helpful to the heart, liver, spleen meridians, in lowering cholesterol, and purges stagnant blood from the uterus.

KEM-Unity - Black Oneness. "Kem" is the Kemetic word that translated into English is "Black". "Unity" is defined in english as "the state or quality of being one".

Maafa - The Afrakan holocaust that has wiped the continent of Africa of over 200 million of it's inhabitants and is still in bloody process as of the time of this writing.

RAspect - The act of seeing divinity or divine light. "Ra" = "Divine Light" ; "Spect" = to "see"

KWK - "Katha Wa Katha". This term translates into english as "and so forth" and can be likened to the Latin "etcetera".

Egun - Yoruba term translated into english as Ancestors

Lidlotis - Bantu term translated into english as Ancestors

Nananom Nsamanfo - Akan term translated into english as *Revered* Ancestors (plural)

14 Afrakan Principles - The "Nguzo Saba" and the "7 Prin-

GLOSSARY

ciples of Ma'at" (see below).

Nguzo Saba - 7 principles for Nation Building offered to the Afrakan Come-unity by Dr. Maulana Karenga.

The principles are as follows:

Umoja (Unity)

To strive for and maintain unity in the family, community, nation and race.

Kujichagulia (Self-Determination)

To define ourselves, name ourselves, create for ourselves and speak for ourselves.

Ujima (Collective Work and Responsibility)

To build and maintain our community together and make our brother's and sister's problems our problems and to solve them together.

Ujamaa (Cooperative Economics)

To build and maintain our own stores, shops and other businesses and to profit from them together.

Nia (Purpose)

To make our collective vocation the building and developing of our community in order to restore our people to their traditional greatness.

Kuumba (Creativity)

To do always as much as we can, in the way we can, in order to leave our community more beautiful and beneficial than we inherited it.

Imani (Faith)

To believe with all our heart in our people, our parents, our teachers, our leaders and the righteousness and victory of our struggle.

Ma'at - Feminine deity from the Kemetic Pantheon of the Ntchru who embodied what was called the "42 Laws of Ma'at" and the following 7 principles:

Truth, Evenhandedness, Harmony, Balance, Order, Reciprocity, Propriety

---

Notes

Notes

Made in the USA
San Bernardino, CA
06 November 2016